50

Ways to Master Your Sewing Machine

Also by Linda Denner

Baby Quilts: 30 Full-Color Patterns in Patchwork and Appliqué,
Worked by Hand and Machine Quilting

Creative Quilting for Home Decor:
30 Full-Color Patterns in Patchwork and Appliqué,
Worked by Hand and Machine Quilting

Ways to Master Your Sewing Machine

An Operator's Guide
to Sewing Techniques

With 30 Color Original Inspirational Designs

Linda Denner

Photographs by Leonard Denner

CROWN TRADE PAPERBACKS • NEW YORK

Published by Crown Trade Paperbacks, 201 East 50th Street, New York, New York 10022. Member of the Crown Publishing Group.

Random House, Inc. New York, Toronto, London, Sydney, Auckland

CROWN TRADE PAPERBACKS and colophon are trademarks of Crown Publishers, Inc.

Manufactured in Hong Kong

Design by Cynthia Dunne

Library of Congress Cataloging-in-Publication Data

Denner, Linda.
50 ways to master your sewing machine / by Linda Denner; photographs by Leonard Denner.
— 1st pbk. ed.
p. cm.
Includes bibliographical references and index.
1. Machine sewing. 2. Sewing machines. I. Title.
TT713.D46 1996
646.2'44—dc20   95-24072
CIP

ISBN 0-517-88360-0

10 9 8 7 6 5 4 3 2 1

First Edition

For My Beloved Daughters, Diana and Pamela

Contents

Acknowledgments

I would like to express my appreciation to the following companies for their invaluable cooperation:

Bernina of America, 3500 Thayer Court, Aurora, Illinois 60504

Brothers International Corporation, 200 Cottontail Lane, Somerset, New Jersey 08875

Elna Inc., 7642 Washington Avenue South, Eden Prairie, Minnesota 55344

Gutermann of America, P.O. Box 7387, Charlotte, North Carolina 28241

New Home Sewing Machine Company, 100 Hollister Road, Teterboro, New Jersey 07608

Pfaff American Sales, 610 Winters Avenue, Paramus, New Jersey 07653

Rhode Island Textile Company, Rhode Island

Singer Sewing Company, 200 Metroplex Drive, Edison, New Jersey 08818

Sulky of America, 3113-D Broadpoint Dr., Harbor Hills, Florida 33983

Tacony Corporation, 1760 Gilsinn Lane, Fenton, Missouri 63026

The Finishing Touch Thread Company, P.O. Box 890, Land O'Lakes, Florida 34639

Viking Sewing Machine Company, 11760 Berea Road, Cleveland, Ohio 44111

YLI Corporation, P.O. Box 109, Provo, Utah 84603

50

Ways to Master
Your Sewing Machine

Introduction

rdent sewers remember their first sewing machines like adolescents recall a first kiss. My love affair with sewing machines started early in my life and has continued to the present. On Christmas morning when I was eight years old I was presented with a child's Singer sewing machine. It stitched only a chain stitch, but in time I made a variety of clothing for my entire doll family and some basic garments for myself. Three years later I received my grandfather's power machine, a 1905 industrial straight-stitch machine with a one-half horsepower motor. Pop had been a tailor, like all his seven brothers and sisters. Upon his passing, the family decided I was the appropriate recipient of this impressive giant, and my father showed me how to operate it. Forty years later, I recall that this old classic had an extensive array of accessory feet similar to many shown in this book. Eventually we sold this machine to a local cleaning establishment, and it would be no surprise if it is still working today.

The evolution of sewing machines, from simple straight stitch machines to the computerized marvels of today, mirrors the growth of our technology. In the 1850s the introduction of an affordable interlocking straight stitch sewing machine freed women from the drudgery of producing every garment for her household by hand. Today's machines interface with computers, embroider, and produce garments of professional quality. The new generation of sewer is turning to her machine to satisfy a basic drive for individuality and creativity. Computerization provides the accuracy and repeatability to the novice that was previously achieved only through years of experience. A working knowledge of DOS or computer science is not required to master modern sewing machines. Most machine manufacturers provide wonderful manuals and videos. Dealer support should be available to carry the sewer through the steps of learning the machine. Whether you own a new machine or a basic model that has been untouched in a closet for many years, this book is for you.

Most sewers do not use their machines to their full capability. The basic feet and features, when used properly, will save hours of work and provide the professional level of workmanship you can take pride in. Maintenance of your equipment is therefore of the utmost importance. Most service calls, while lucrative to the repairmen, result from operator error. Failure to change the needle, having the incorrect needle for the job, or a machine seized with lint are all common and totally avoidable repairs.

I am here to help you overcome fear of your sewing machine. The only power the machine has, *you* provide with pressure on the foot control. When the machine goes too fast, and you're afraid of it getting away from you, apply less pressure with your foot. If the needle breaks, the machine will survive and so will you! Make sure the tip is out of the bobbin casing, put a new needle in, and start again. Trust me, there is little you can do to your machine to cause complete failure. Just as with our children, we make many mistakes with our sewing machines and they somehow survive. Neglect is machines' worst enemy. Clean them, oil them and READ THE MANUAL.

Through the generosity and cooperation of the major sewing machine manufacturers, eight different brand sewing machines demonstrate the sewing operations featured in this text. It is my hope that while you may not have the specific model machine featured, you will have a machine similar to one of these eight. It is exciting as well to see the variety of wonderful designs that they all offer. Basic features, presser feet and, most importantly, sewing techniques are similar for all sewing machines. I hope that this book will be an aid to help you sew with more success and explore the potential that your machine provides for timesaving and artistic expression.

---- 1 ----

Needles, Thread, and Fabric

Though many years have passed since I took geometry in high school, I still recall laws that were essential. The whole is equal to the sum of its parts is a doctrine I learned those many years ago, and it applies to sewing as well as math. The quality of the stitch that your sewing machine produces is the product not just of the machine and its settings. It shows the skill of the operator, and the quality of the needle, thread, and fabric.

NEEDLES

You may be fortunate to own a new computerized sewing machine, but with a dull needle it will sew a poor quality stitch. There is no reward in heaven for the sewer who is using the oldest sewing machine needle. No single component will influence the outcome of your work more dramatically than having a sharp, appropriate size needle for the job. When beginning a project, change the needle on your sewing machine. If you see skipped stitches, or poorly formed stitches, change the needle. Before you take your machine in to a repairman to look for the cause of its poor performance, *change your needle.* As the world of sewing has changed in the past years, the types of needles manufactured has changed as well. I know that you recall a time when you used the same needle, perhaps a size 14/90 for every fabric. In those days the fabrics were all natural; however, with today's manmade textiles you need needles to complement construction.

There are several features that determine the design and purpose of a sewing machine needle. The thickness of the needle dictates the weight of fabric that it will pierce with a minimal hole, and the shape of the point will help or hinder the fabric penetration. A sharp point will insure perfectly straight stitches, and be most appropriate for a finely woven fiber such as pima cotton, silk, or microfibers (a generic term for *manmade*). A ballpoint needle has a rounded tip that will slide between the fibers of a knit without catching and pulling on the threads. A universal needle has a tip that is somewhat rounded yet sharp at the same time, and will perform correctly for most of your general sewing.

Specialty needle designs have been developed to handle the new fabrics and threads. Attempt repair or construction of a pair of jeans and you'll understand the need for a needle to help do the job. Jeans needles have tips that are chiselled in shape and penetrate the densely woven denim without problems. If you found your sewing machine inadequate for repairing jeans, it may not have been the machine, but the needle. Stretch needles are made for synthetic suedes and elastic knitwear; these prevent skipped stitches when sewing these fabrics. Leather needles have a slight cutting point for leather and heavy nonwoven synthetics like vinyl or laminates. These will turn a difficult sewing problem into a routine operation.

If you have had problems with rayon or metallic thread breaking as you stitch, try resolving this with topstitching or metallic needles. Extra-sharp, with an extra-large eye, these needles accommodate specialty thread without shredding or breaking it. Needles are constructed with a groove running down the front that cradles the thread as it carries it through the fibers of the material. The topstitching or metallic needle has a deeper groove to accommodate the thicker synthetic decorative threads that prevents thread breakage as the stitch is formed. An additional bonus to this needle is the wonderfully large-sized eye. If you have mature eyesight, you will find this needle a joy to thread. You may decide that this needle will solve your threading problems and use it for most woven fabrics. For sight-impaired sewers there is a self-threading needle with a slot for snapping the thread into the eye.

I enjoy machine quilting and in the past used universal 80/12 needle for this purpose. The synthetic battings tend to dull the needle. The free-motion stitch operation bends the needle as well. The new quilting needles, specifically designed with a special taper to the point, aid in the penetration of the layers and maintain their sharpness longer. The needle groove is deep and carries the thread, protecting against snagging and breakage. This needle also permits the use of decorative metallic thread in your quilting.

The size of the needle is noted by two numbers: the American sizing followed by the European sizing (which parallels wire gauge). The size of the needle refers to its thickness, and the size is selected according to the weight of your fabric. The following chart relates the needle size to fabric weight and the most common usage for these specifications.

The wing needle was developed to create a hemstich in fabric. The needle has a blade-like construction on either side of the shaft. The needle tip size is either 100 or 120. On tightly woven fabrics the needle can be used to create openwork for decorative effects. A double-hemstitch needle is available, which is composed of one wing needle and one regular needle joined on a single shaft. The double-hemstitch needle may also be used for decorative stitching and requires a zigzag sewing machine. The throat plate of a straight-stitch sewing machine will not allow for the clearance of the wider needle shaft.

Twin needles in this book perform several operations, from pintucking to topstitching. They are two needles joined by a cross-bar from a single shaft. They can be used on any zigzag sewing machine that threads from front to back. The size and purpose will follow the chart below. An additional reference will be noted on these needles, which is the width of the distance between the needles. Check the zigzag and throat plate opening available for your specific sewing machine before purchasing twin needles. The throat plate opening must be large enough to accommodate the passage of the two needles. The wider the distance between the two needles, the heavier weight fabric they will accommodate. The bobbin side of a twin needle seam will always be a zigzag. The needles will share the same bobbin thread. When topstitching with twin needles, eliminate fabric tunneling between the needles by using a Wooley Nylon thread in the bobbin. This thread will stretch between the rows of stitching and allow the topstitching to lie flat.

Many sewing machines have a twin needle key selection that, when engaged, will prevent needle breakage if you are executing a zigzag or decorative stitch. Refer to your machine manual or confer with the dealer to determine how this key operates.

Some manufacturers will halve the size of the stitch width when the twin needle is engaged, and other companies (such as Pfaff) reduce the

Needle Size	Fabric Weight	Construction Type
9/65; 10/70, 11/75	lightweight woven or knit fibers	lingerie, heirloom, and bridal sewing
12/80	dress-weight cottons and knits	garment construction piecing and appliqué
14/90	denim, corduroy, canvas, and upholstery fabrics	garment construction, home decorating
100/16	backed decorative fabric (such as herculon), fake fur	toys, garment construction
110/18;120/10 Commonly found in wing needles	purposely creating a hole for decorative use	hemstitching, fagoting, embellishing

size of the stitch width by one millimeter on either side of the stitch width pattern. Ascertaining this factor for your machine will allow you to alter stitch programs even when you are not working with a twin needle. Certain model Bernina sewing machines halve the width of their patterns when the twin needle key is engaged. Knowing this allows you to reduce all your decorative stitches by 50 percent when stitching with or without twin needles.

A needle for decorative stitching, new at this writing, is a triple needle. This needle conforms to the size chart, and is limited to use on a zigzag, front-threading sewing machine. In using this needle I found it critical for all three threads to be the same weight and thread type. If you use two spools of cotton thread and one rayon, your stitch formation on the rayon thread will be loopy and not conform to the other two stitched rows. Uniformity of thread will correct this problem.

As time goes on and more fabrics and threads are introduced to the home sewers, more needle types will appear. Don't be skeptical of their value, rather check to see if there is a specific needle for your needs. Sewing machine companies do not manufacture needles. They are made by major needle manufacturers and packaged under a wide variety of names. Needle manufacturers make two types of needles, home sewing machine needles and industrial sewing machine needles. If you own a home sewing machine, you can utilize all the many brands like Schmetz, Singer, Bernina, Pfaff, Organ, or John Doe needles. Check with the dealer if they are home sewing machine needles, and buy them with confidence.

(Also see photographic Sequence 32—Needles, p. 91.)

THREAD

Returning to the geometric principle that the whole is only as good as the sum of its parts, thread becomes crucial to sewing success. What does a sewing machine really do? It takes a threaded needle through the surface of cloth that is caught by a hook within the bobbin and secured with a knot to create a stitch. The cloth is then moved forward at a set rate via the feed dogs of your machine, and this operation is repeated again and again. The knots lie between the layers of fibers, and will hopefully integrate inconspicuously within the weave and texture. Since the function of the machine is to make knots, it therefore follows that the thread is of the utmost importance. Old thread that has weakened with age will produce a weak knot. Bargain priced thread more than likely has manufacturing deficiencies. It may be irregularly spun, not shrink resistant, or lack elasticity. Purchase good thread, and dispose of those old cones that your Great-Aunt Millie passed on in the family.

Keep in mind the knots that we are creating as we sew, and it logically follows that the finer the fabric the finer the knots we require for the stitches to be inconspicuously incorporated into the fabric weave. Cotton fibers will produce the finest knots (or stitches), and will be your best choice for fine-weight natural fabrics. Thread is composed of two filaments that are twisted together into what is referred to as a two-ply thread. The filament weight is referred to as the denier, and theoretically should be based on a standard weight of 5 centimeters per 450 meters of silk. Unfortunately filament weights vary among manufacturers. What one company designates 50 weight another may call 40. The weight of these threads is noted on the spools; 50 weight is usual for common sewing construction. The lower the number, the thicker the thread. Coats & Clark's produces a fine weight of 40 for lightweight fabrics. Use a size 60 or 70 needle in your machine for a lightweight thread.

Years ago sewing was done on natural fibers and cotton thread was the thread of choice. Today with synthetic fibers added to natural, as well as man-made blended fabrics, polyester threads are most appropriate. The widest color selection is available in polyester, the thread allows for stretch, and resists deterioration when exposed to the elements. Polyester thread is unaffected by many chemicals used in leather tanning and Fiber-Etch (the product used for cutwork). In most construction the strength of the seam is increased with the use of polyester thread.

Silk thread is the strongest and costliest thread of all. It is produced for home sewers for use in hand stitching and tailoring details. My grandfather was a tailor and he used silk thread in men's coats and wool suits for strength. "The seam would outlive the garment," reassured Pop, and I am certain he was correct. For a silk garment, this thread would be too strong and cut into the fibers. Silk buttonhole twist is a wonderful accent for topstitching a coat or garment. This is a heavier weight thread with the high sheen we love about silk and wound on small spools, each holding as little as 30 yards of thread.

With the increased interest in machine embroidery, we are seeing a growing array of rayon thread. Rayon has a sheen like silk and takes dyes wonderfully. Rayon is not a strong fiber, like cotton or polyester; however, strength is not a factor when stitching a lined embroidery pattern or a densely embroidered motif. Rayon thread is available in 30- and 40-weight threads. Problems may arise when a pattern is increased in scale and the rayon thread fails to fill the enlarged motif. A new thread company, The Finishing Touch Thread Company listed in the acknowledgments of this book, manufactures a 30-weight rayon high quality thread that will fill all patterns. This thread is made of a two-ply 150 denier thread while other companies' 30-weight is made of a 120 denier two-ply. The heavier weight thread is available in over eighty colors, and will provide sufficient coverage for embroidery bed sewing machines and enlarged line embroidery found in standard sewing machines.

Metallic thread is available for decorative stitchery, and is constructed of a metallic thread wrapped around a rayon core thread. The weight number is deleted from the spool notation, and will vary from brand to brand and color to color. Experimentation will determine which will best suit your needs. The dye action on this thread will affect its strength. Within one manufacturer's line I have had great success with all their metallic shades with the exception of green. Green dyes are quite caustic in fabric, and I have observed that many green metallic threads suffer from the same weakness. Certain fiber dyes also have a tendency to attract more static electricity that results in twisting and thread breakage. Spool rings made of a plastic styrofoam material placed on the spool holder in front and behind the spool will take the static electricity out of the thread. They furthermore stop the spool from turning and keep the thread from getting caught under or behind the spool.

Select a topstitching needle when using rayon or metallic thread to prevent the breakage and separation of the ply. Metallic and rayon threads are designed for decorative work and are inappropriate for garment construction seams.

The cost factor of decorative threads is important. To minimize the injury to your pocketbook and to facilitate the best use for your sewing machine, use bobbin/lingerie thread. This thread comes in light and dark opaque colors and is half the weight of decorative threads. Fill the bobbin of your sewing machine with this thread, and your bobbin will load with double its normal amount of thread. Lighten the needle tension two numbers, which will allow the needle thread to remain on the surface of the fabric and prevent the bobbin thread from showing on the surface. This eliminates having to wind bobbins in numerous matching colors, and you will need to purchase far less thread of one color.

A cone stand will be an invaluable aid for using a wide variety of threads on your machine. You will need this for using oversized spools or feeding spools that present problems when placed on your machine's spool holder. A cone holder can eliminate the problem of spool backlash if your machine has a vertical spool holder. This problem occurs when the thread intermittently spins the plastic spool resulting in tangled thread on the bobbin side of your seam. Winding a bobbin of decorative thread, such as Pearl Crown rayon or Ribbon Floss™ can be successfully accomplished with a cone holder.

If a thread is too thick to pass through the needle's eye, you have two options. You can wind the thread on the bobbin of your machine or you can couch the thread on the surface of the fabric. (See the Couching Sequence, p. 54.) This type of embroidery is referred to as "bobbin work." Most heavy threads packaged for this purpose will wind on the bobbin without difficulty. Since they are heavier, the bobbin will hold less and it would be advisable to wind several bobbins at one time. Place the bobbin in your bobbin case and test the tension of the thread as it is pulled out of the case. For drop-in bobbins pull the thread end, advancing the thread past the spring mechanism into the slot opening. For a front-loading bobbin case, a spare bobbin case is a good investment. A front-loading bobbin case has two screws on the case, one large and one small-sized screw. The large one is the one to adjust with a small screwdriver. Remember the axiom, "Righty tighty, lefty loosey." Move the screw to the left no more than a quarter turn.

Pull on the heavy thread until it comes off the bobbin with a similar resistance as ordinary thread pulls out of the threaded bobbin case.

Select a straight stitched motif, not a pattern made of a satin stitch formation. Indeed, a straight stitch will serve you well for this operation. Draw a pattern on stabilizer and position this on the wrong side of your fabric. (See the Fabrics section for a discussion of stabilizers.) Using thread in the needle to match the bobbin thread, straight stitch on the wrong side of your cloth, following the lines on your stabilizer drawing. Allow extra long ends when cutting your thread to allow you to pull the heavy weight to the wrong side of your cloth to tie off. On the right side of your fabric the motif will be sewn with the decorative bobbin work. This technique is a particular favorite of mine as it can be accomplished with any sewing machine even if that machine can only perform a straight stitch. The only requirement for the operator is the ability to sew on a lined drawing—we can all do that!

The last type thread that I would like to encourage you to try is the wonderful assortment of variegated threads in either cotton, metallic, or rayon fibers. On the spool these threads may be unimpressive. Sewed out, the threads create repeatable bands of color blocks that are captivating. In rows of satin-stitch scallops or straight stitch, this thread will add pizzazz.

For selecting thread color, bring a swatch of the fabric to the fabric store for reference. The thread color will look darker on the spool than if you hold one strand up to the material. When sewing two colors or shades of fabric together you should select the darker of the two colors.

FABRIC

I do not believe that there is a sewer alive that requires any encouragement to purchase fabric. Most of us buy yardage as though the manufacturers plan to halt production at any moment. I don't know about you, but I for one can hold out for several decades on what's already in my closet! I pretreat my fabric by either laundering or steam pressing according to the fabric type before construction. I do not want the garment to shrink after I have painstakingly seen to its proper fit.

The topic that I feel is vital to your sewing success is stabilizers. We were all delighted when the dealer demonstrated the wonderful stitching capability of our sewing machine models upon purchase. He happily stitched away on either pink or white cloth and scallops and buttonholes looked terrific—better than they ever appeared when the machine came to reside at our home. Was it all done with mirrors? Or perhaps it was a trick demonstrator model only found in the dealer showroom. The answer to this puzzle is the demonstration cloth used at the time of the sale of your machine. Dealers use a highly starched cloth, called demo cloth, to display a machine's features. The cloth must be sufficiently stiff to support dense stitchery on a single layer. At home you may have used tissue paper when stitching a buttonhole, but this weight is far too light. I have listed here some stabilizer options. Interfacing the area is sometimes the correct option, but there may be times when the stitchery requires a stabilizer as well as interfacing, and the more common scenario will be when you want to avoid the interfacing altogether. The proper stabilizer for the task will restore your confidence in the quality and capability of your machine.

There are many stabilizers made by various manufacturers that are placed under the cloth and are easily torn off when the stitching is completed. Under the names Stitch and Tear or Tear-Away, these products are inexpensive in cost and will be the type you use the most frequently. They are intended for light- to medium-weight fabrics and will support all thicknesses of embroidery and construction details such as buttonholes. In ready-made garments the tear-away stabilizers are frequently left in the garments and will survive many washings. For the sewer, removal will prevent stiffness as well as irritation to the skin.

"Totally Stable" by Sulky is a iron-on stabilizer that eliminates stretching and sliding of the fabric. This is suitable for knits or slippery fabric.

If your concern is ease of removal of the stabilizer when working with a fragile fabric, there are products that fall away when heat is applied. This is a nice option for cutwork where the stabilizer will provide the support for the stitchery, yet dissolve with the heat of the iron. The use of a pressing cloth is recommended when the heat may be damaging to delicate fabric. A new and exciting stabilizer available is "Firm Hold" from The Finishing Touch Thread Company. This product is a press-on stabilizer with a polymer-coated side. When heat is applied, the polymers form a plug between the threads of the fabric and become as one with the fabric. When cool, the Firm Hold will pull away without leaving any of the residue of the product on the fabric. This allows chiffon and lace to be as carefree to embroider as starched linen.

When embroidering lace fabric or tulle, use a wash-away plastic stabilizer. You may find this packaged under the name "Solvy"™ or "Wash-A-Way"™. Put one layer under the thin fabric, and one layer on top. Hoop the layers, even for embroidery designs feed by your machine, since holding the layers firmly will help in the stitch formation. When the stitchery is completed, tear away the excess plastic, storing it in a plastic bag. Spray the residue with water and the remainder will dissolve, leaving your embroidery clear yet starched. The waste sections can be dissolved with water and used as a starch to spot stabilize. With a sufficient quantity of excess Solvy you can submerge cloth for a heavily starched cloth similar in weight to demonstration cloth. This fabric would then be suitable for supporting stitchery without a stabilizer.

A relatively new product is "Perfect Sew." If you wish to spot-stabilize an area or create your own entre-deux, brush a small amount of this solution on your fabric and allow it to dry. You may facilitate the drying with a blow-dryer and iron. Perfect Sew can be spread on the surface of the cloth using a small stenciling sponge. Select a decorative stitch, loosen the needle tension, and sew. This product works equally well on wovens and knits. Perfect Sew will completely wash out when the garment is laundered.

Freezer paper is an inexpensive and useful stabilizer for many sewing projects. With the paper backing you may trace your design for reverse operations. The plastic coating will bond to the wrong side of the cloth when a medium hot iron is applied. This is suitable for knits as well as wovens.

The last, yet not the least stabilizer is delivered to our door free of charge daily: junk mail. The correct weight for a stabilizer is the weight of common computer paper. Recycle these products when sewing for most of your stabilizing needs. The additional weight of the paper will cause no harm to the machine. The needle will dull with or without the paper as you work with the many decorative stitches. Change the width and length or the patterns as you experiment. Explore the utility stitches as well as the specific decorative programs.

When beginning a project, experiment with the various stabilizers available on the fabric you are using. Explore the variety, as there is no one product that will accommodate all situations. Your directions may call for you to interface your garment, but it will still need a stabilizer for certain operations like stitching buttonholes. This is no reflection on the quality of the machine. Stabilize when using a new computerized dream machine or if you are sewing with grandma's black-headed antique.

2

Machine Problems and Solutions

 am not a late night sewer. I can begin most projects in the morning with energy and a clear head. This is not possible for many who must approach sewing at the end of a busy day. Regrettably, fatigue compounds small errors leading to an unsatisfactory experience. To ease tension, set realistic goals for your work period. An hour of productive time is better than two with time spent ripping out new construction. For most of us sewing is a relaxing outlet. Quit when you are frustrated or too tired to continue.

Upon purchasing your sewing machine, avail yourself of every opportunity for machine instruction. If monthly clubs are featured at the dealership, be certain to attend. The topic may not be of immediate interest, but each session will expose you to confidence-building machine techniques. Read the machine manual periodically, and have it ready for quick reference. If the manual has been lost, contact the dealer or manufacturer to obtain a new manual. Most manufacturers provide a toll-free telephone number for consumer information. Trained technicians will cheerfully talk through your problems Monday through Friday. If your brand is generic, learn the manufacturer for added support. *The Creative Machine Newsletter,* listed in the bibliography of this book, is an excellent source for obtaining machine information. This magazine networks consumer problems and questions of each sewing machine brand and model. With restricted advertising, this publication provides an objective review of all sewing-related products.

To avoid difficulty, always work with good thread and change the needle to an appropriate size at the beginning of every sewing project. Oil your machine with sewing machine oil for every eight hours of running time. This oil is light in weight and evaporates as you sew. Replenishing the oil eliminates noise and the risk of a seized machine. If your machine is stored in a cold area, it will require warming up time for proper performance. Bring the machine to a heated room, put its light on, and run the unthreaded machine for about ten minutes. Add a drop of oil to the race of the machine if it has been idle for some time. If you plan decorative stitching that may require adjustment, balance the stitch after the machine has run for several minutes. As the machine oils start to flow, stitch quality improves. (See Sequence 11, Cleaning and Oiling, p. 49.)

Thread entanglements occur on the opposite side of the cloth than the problem's origin. A bird's nest on the underside of the cloth suggests a problem along the needle threading path. The following chart contains problems and frequent solutions. One or more of the suggestions should correct your difficulty. Trial and error with a touch of patience will save the day.

PROBLEMS	SOLUTIONS
Bobbin thread showing on surface	Decrease needle tension or increase tension on bobbin case.
Fabric not feeding	Raise feed dogs. Lengthen stitch.
Fabric puckering	Shorten stitch length. Needle point may be dull,
	change needle. Pfaff owners, engage dual-feed. Stabilize.
Foot-pedal moving	Lay rubberized material under foot control.
Machine jamming	Clear out threads under throat plate and bobbin case. Clean, brush bobbin area. Rethread. Pull threads to the rear when beginning.
Machine moving	Place thin rubber mat under machine to absorb movement and noise.
Machine noisy	Change needle. Remove built up thread under throat plate. Oil.
Machine not on	Check plugs if set in correctly. Check switches.
Machine not sewing	Fly-wheel may be disengaged. Bobbin winding mechanism still engaged.
Metallic thread breaking	Use topstitching needle. Apply Sewer's Aid to spool.
Needle breaking	Incorrect needle size used. Change to appropriate size needle. Thread entangled on cone. Correctly insert bobbin case. Insert needle completely.
Poor quality buttonhole	Stabilize cloth. Trim seam allowance bulk away. Position buttonhole lengthwise on fabric grain to eliminate stretch and distortion. Use buttonhole foot.

Poor quality decorative stitch	Use correct presser foot. Stabilize fabric. Lighten needle tension about two settings. Dull needle or burr within needle eye; change needle.
Poor quality straight stitch	Use correct foot. Balance tension. Increase pressure. Decrease stitch length.
Sheer fabric drawn into thread	Stabilize fabric. Use straight stitch foot and then straight stitch throat plate.
Spool spinning	Use cone holder or extend the holder by inserting a drinking straw over the spool pin. Position spool rings on side of thread.
Thread not covering embroidery motif	Use heavier weight 40 rayon thread.
Throat plate drawing in lightweight fabric	Stitch presser foot and straighten throat plate.
Skipped stitches	Dull needle. Change needle to appropriate type and size. Bobbin may be low. Use Sewer's Aid™ on spool.
Uneven stitches	Do not pull fabric from back when stitching. Gently guide cloth from front. Increase presser foot pressure.
Unthreading	Raise take-up lever position before sewing. Cut thread ends about 6" long. Needle incorrectly inserted.

The above procedures will address the day-to-day minor difficulties sewers must expect as routine. Perform regular maintenance as detailed in our sequence on oiling and cleaning your machine. When a problem arises, carefully cut jammed threads away and clean out the problem area. Lint and a dull needle are the most frequent causes of machine trouble.

You can easily address these problems. Make sure to have your machine checked annually by an authorized dealer. The lubrication and cleaning the dealer will provide will ensure years of service for your machine.

3

Photographic Machine Techniques

**T**he sewing machine techniques featured in this chapter were executed on a variety of machine brands and models. They are the top of the line models from the major manufacturers. It is fascinating to see the latest technology in this field. Remember, however, that all sewing machines are alike in their basic function. They create an interlocking stitch in fabric. Electronic and computerized enhancements replace operator skill to a very large degree. They increase accuracy and insure repeatable results. It is a rare sewer that believes she uses her machine to full capacity. Owning a new machine marvel does not guarantee the operator will not use it exactly like her previous straight-stitch model. What we all need to do is invest the time to explore the stitch capacity of our own machine. Small but significant adjustments will make the difference from failure to success. Alphabetically, in photographic sequence, techniques and operations are presented for your convenience.

1. Satin stitch machine appliqué requires a zigzag sewing machine.

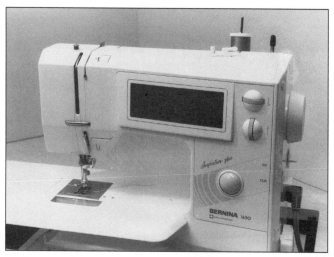

2. Use an open appliqué foot for maximum visibility. The foot provides a wide channel on the underside that allows smooth passage of the satin stitching. Wind the bobbin of the sewing machine with lingerie/bobbin thread.

3. Lighten the needle setting on your machine two numbers, or to a buttonhole tension setting. Use the lingerie/bobbin thread to wind all the bobbins thus eliminating the need of winding matching-color bobbins. This thread is lightweight allowing the bobbin conveniently to hold twice the amount of thread. With a lightened tension the satin stitching lies on the surface of the cloth in a more pleasing formation.

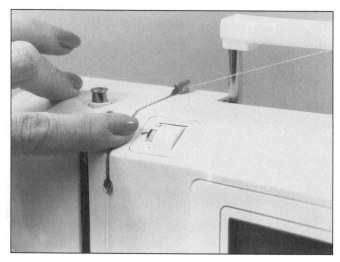

4. Use a fusible web material, and iron the appliqué to the background fabric. Position a stabilizer behind the wrong side of your cloth before beginning.

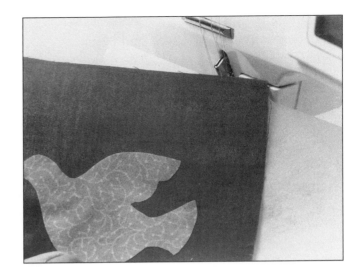

5. Position the needle on the outside edge of the appliqué, and adjust the needle to swing into the appliqué. All the satin stitches should fall within the appliqué. Select a medium zigzag 2 mm–3 mm wide, and a short stitch length.

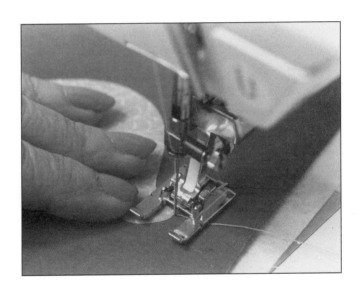

6. Curves are kept smooth by frequently pivoting the foot. Keep the needle in the cloth when raising the presser foot. Reposition the work to maintain the satin stitches along the raw edge of the appliqué. If your sewing machine has a needle-down option, engage this feature when pivoting.

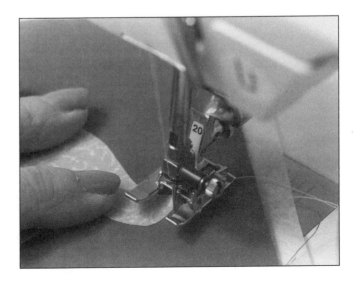

7. Complete the satin stitching to the end of a corner. Lift the presser foot, and begin the line of satin stitching parallel to the new raw edge. This row of stitches will be just under the previous completed row as shown.

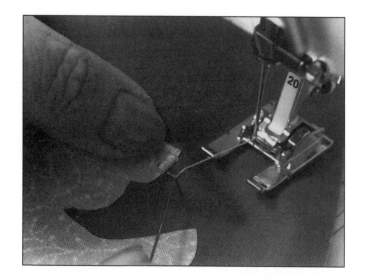

8. Your completed appliqué will be consistent in stitch quality if you frequently pivot the work and use a stabilizer.

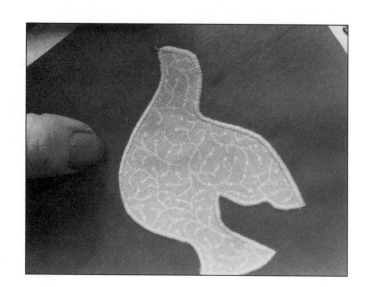

9. Experiment with filled decorative stitches in addition to a basic satin stitch. The fusible web secured the appliqués sufficiently for the edge to be worked with a wide variety of programs.

10. After completion, remove the stabilizer from the wrong side of the cloth.

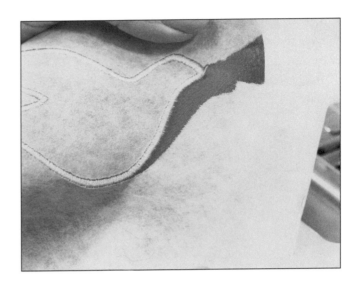

SEQUENCE 2—BASTING

1. Frequently refer to the sewing machine manual or the built-in sewing advisor your machine may offer. Familiarize yourself with the machine controls for tension, pressure, stitch length, width, and speed options. The controls will allow for basic operations and beyond.

2. Select a straight stitch foot for most construction seams and basting. Note the bottom of the straight stitch foot is smooth. The foot on the left is grooved for the passage of zigzagging. This is a multipurpose foot or zigzag foot.

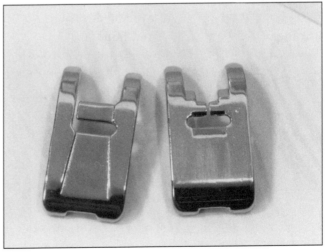

3. Select a stitch length of 3 mm and change the needle tension to a low setting of two to three.

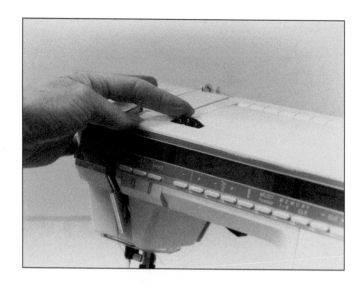

4. Sew the fabric on the seamline.

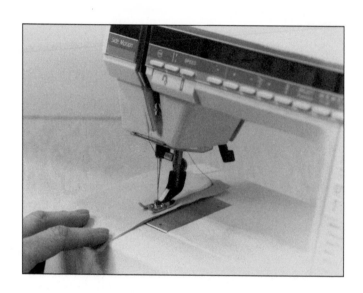

5. The 3 mm stitch length is a secure stitch. It will prevent the seams unravelling during a fitting.

6. The light needle tension allows the bobbin to pull the knots to the wrong side of the cloth, creating an unbalanced stitch. Pull the bobbin thread, on the wrong side of the seam, and the thread will easily come out without the need of a seam ripper.

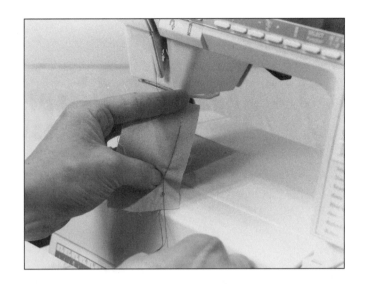

SEQUENCE 3—BEADING

1. A beading or sequin foot is available through your dealership. Generic feet are sold to fit low shank, high shank, and slant foot models. The distinguishing feature of a beading presser foot is a deeply grooved channel for the beads.

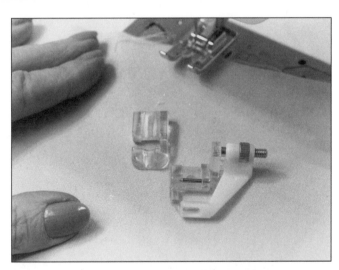

2. Sequins can be attached with a foot, as shown, that provides an opening in front of the needle. The foot guides the trim as it is couched to the background fabric.

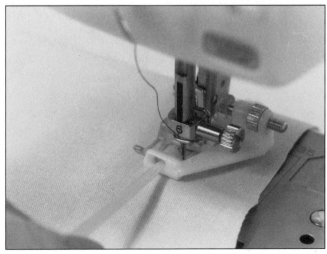

3. Use thread matching the background or nylon monofilament thread. Select a zigzag stitch wider than the bead, and a stitch length consistent with the bead length. After attachment, remove the cloth and manipulate the cloth until the stitches fall under the beads. The stitches shown are sewn in a dark contrasting thread to enhance visibility.

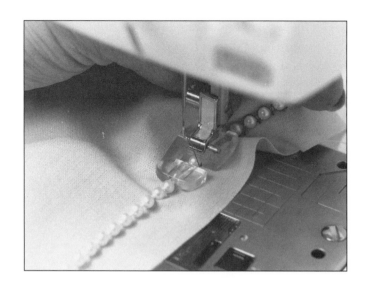

SEQUENCE 4—BINDING

1. An excellent and often neglected attachment is the multi-slotted binder. This foot folds the binding as the machine sews through all the layers.

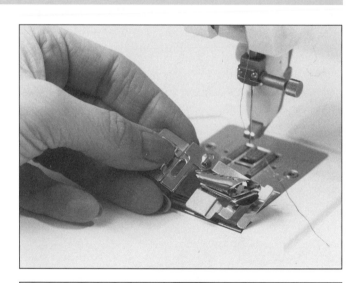

2. Cut the binding ends with a 45-degree angle as shown to reduce a bulky seam. Strips cut 1½" wide are standard to commercial bias. The attachment easily handles this size.

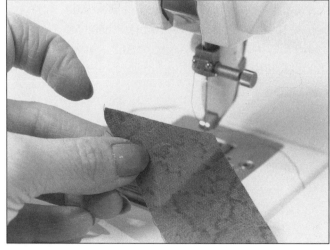

3. With the aid of a pin, slide the binding through the funnel in the foot front. Center the fabric, with an even amount adjusted to either side.

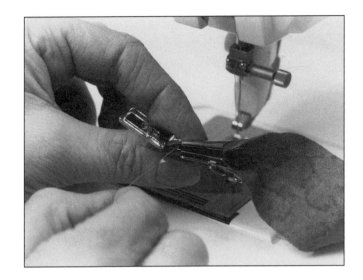

4. Before sewing, pull a sufficient amount of binding through the foot and to the rear of the feed dogs. This allows smooth feeding as you begin.

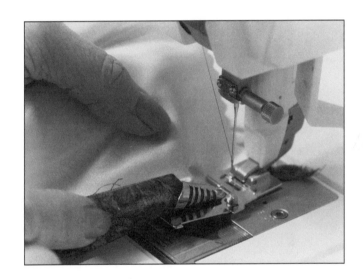

5. The binding is evenly folding and stitched in one operation. Select a straight stitch or zigzag according to the needle opening in the foot.

1. Medium- to heavy-weight fabrics are ideal candidates for a machine blind hem. Measure and fold the hem the depth required.

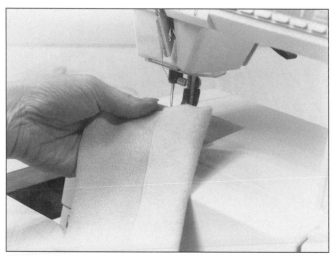

2. Lighten the needle tension two numbers below the normal setting. The wide zigzag stitch formed with the light tension will press flat when the hem is completed.

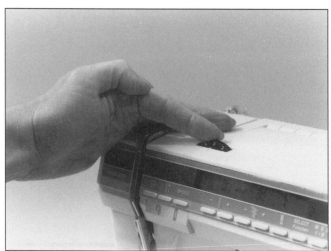

3. Fold the hem back revealing the top underside edge of the hem. Pin as shown, maintaining an even depth. The pin placement will not interfere with the feed dogs, and need not be removed until the end.

4. Use the presser foot recommended by your sewing machine manual for this task. The blind hem presser foot frequently has a lip or wheel that rests against the fold of the hem. The guide conveniently maintains an even sewing path.

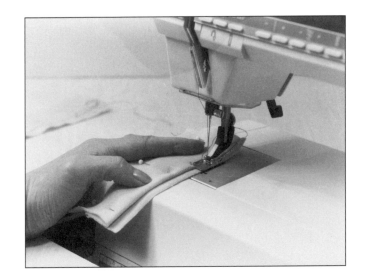

5. The blindstitch shown consists of four straight stitches sewn to the right of the needle. The fifth stitch is a zigzag that swings to the left and into the garment body. The zigzag width is adjustable for different weight fabrics.

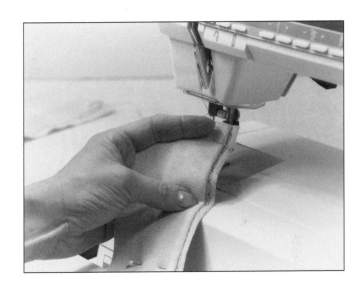

6. Sew a sample with the fashion fabric to decide the zigzag width. With the proper width, you will catch the fabric securely on the left while the seam will be unnoticeable on the right side of the garment. Use matching colored thread when sewing a blind hem. Lighten the needle tension to allow the hem to lay flat when completed.

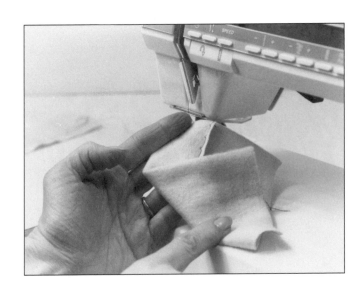

7. On the wrong side of the garment, the blind hem stitch will be most noticeable along the hem fold.

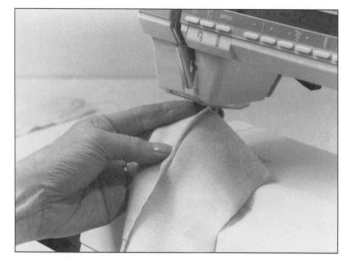

8. Many sewing machines today offer two blind-hem stitches. The stitch shown has a sequence of four narrow zigzags to the right of the needle, with one wide zigzag swinging to the left side of the needle. This blind hem duplicates the finish offered by a serger or overlock machine, and eliminates the folded hem. When the blind hem is completed, trim the hem edge even to the stitching line. The short zigzags finish the raw edge of the fabric.

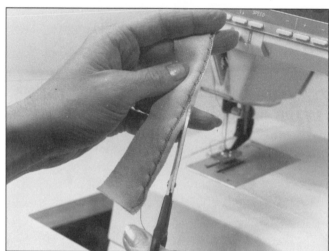

1. This operation mimics the strength and appearance of hand appliqué. Cut appliqués, adding a seam allowance of one-quarter inch. Prepare the appliqués by hand basting or ironing the seam allowance to the wrong side. Press and position the appliqué to the background fabric.

2. Use a tear-away or heat-away stabilizer for additional support for the background fabric.

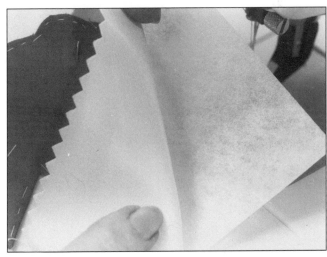

3. Choose the basic blind-hem stitch combining straight stitches with one zigzag. Select matching colored thread or nylon monofilament thread in the needle. Shorten the stitch length to 1.5–2.5 mm, which will create stitches at frequent intervals to anchor the appliqué securely. Adjust the bite of the zigzag to just enter the tip of the appliqué. An open toe (pictured) or clear plastic foot will be best for this task. Position the needle just to the outside right edge of the appliqué, with the straight stitches falling on the background cloth.

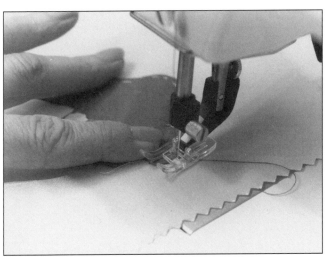

4. When stitching is completed, remove the basting stitches within the appliqué.

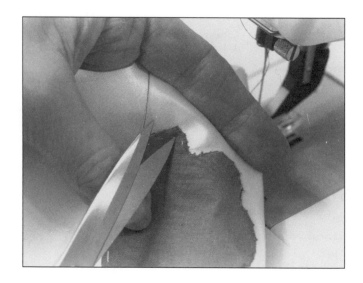

5. Pull away the stabilizer from the wrong side.

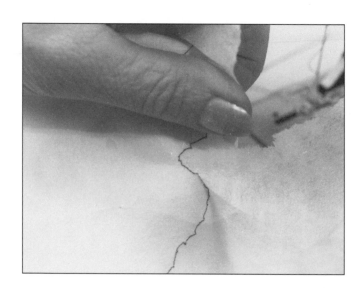

6. Cut away the background fabric that remains under the appliqués. Maintain a ¼" seam allowance when trimming. This eliminates excess bulk under the appliqués. The background fabric color will not show through the appliqués.

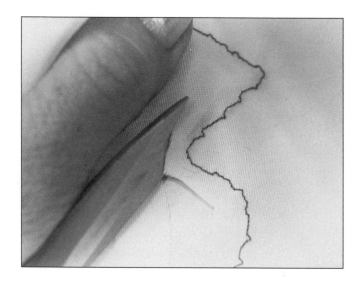

7. With a bit of practice this method will provide the look of hand stitching. Only close examination will reveal the machine work.

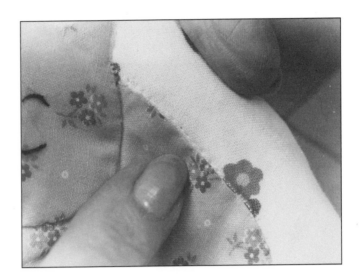

SEQUENCE 7—BOBBIN WORK EMBROIDERY

1. Heavyweight embroidery threads commonly used in overlock or sergers can be used for decorative sewing on your home sewing machine.

2. By hand or machine, wind a bobbin with the heavyweight thread. Adjust the bobbin case by turning the large screw of the case until the thread pulls out easily with similar resistance to that of ordinary sewing thread. Turn the screw to the left to loosen, the right to tighten. Move the screw not more than a quarter turn at a time. For drop-in bobbins, advance the heavy thread past the metal groove to the cut-out opening of the bobbin case.

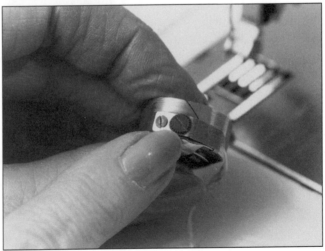

3. Mark the stabilizer with a motif. Use quilting templates or trace a design as shown.

4. Match the needle thread to the bobbin thread color, and sew on the wrong side of the cloth. Begin with a straight stitch on your marked lines. Thread tails can be brought to the wrong side and secured with a knot.

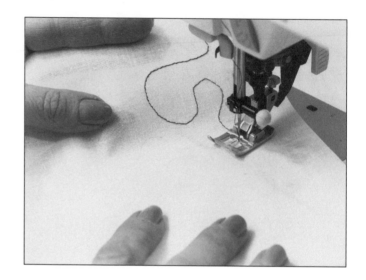

5. On the right side of the cloth, the heavy bobbin thread will be forming the design. For clarity the needle thread shown here is contrasting in color. Increase the needle tension to secure the bobbin embroidery.

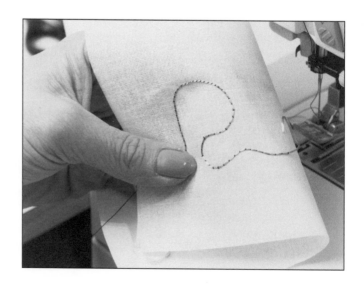

6. The example shown uses Ribbon Floss in the bobbin. It is worked in a variety of colors on gray velvet. This vest is featured in the color section of the book.

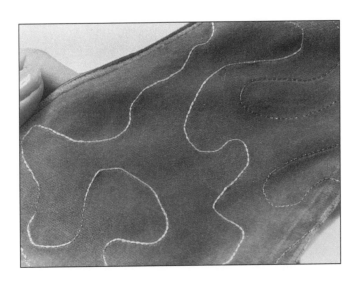

1. Buttonholes vary according to style and function. Fabric properties decide the buttonhole style. A woven fabric will require a satin-stitched buttonhole, while a stretch fabric requires elasticity in the buttonhole formation. Refer to your machine manual for the appropriate selection.

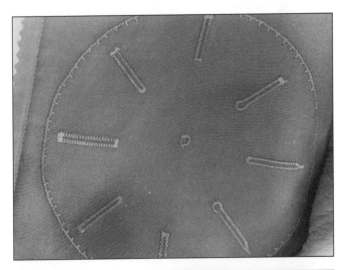

2. Machines vary in the method of measuring buttonhole length. Some machines mechanically measure the button length; others count stitches or sew a preset length selected by the operator. Familiarize yourself with your machine's operation.

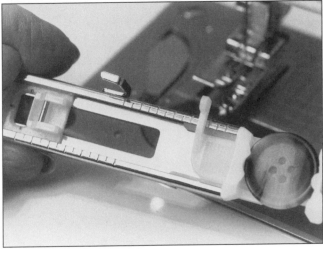

3. Stabilize the cloth whenever making a buttonhole. Interfacing positioned on the wrong side of the garment is insufficient for supporting a buttonhole. Mark the buttonhole placement after the garment is completed.

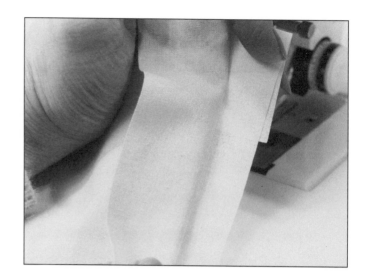

4. Reduce the needle tension two numbers, or to the lighter setting suggested for buttonholes. Sew a sample on the fashion fabric consistent to the size and grain of the garment, with a piece of your chosen stabilizer in place. Buttonholes on woven and knit fabrics are best sewn parallel to the center front edge to eliminate stretch. Test a button after cutting the opening. The button should enter smoothly without distorting the stitches. Put the buttonholes on the garment from the lower edge up. Your buttonholes will improve with practice, and your best will thus fall at the top position.

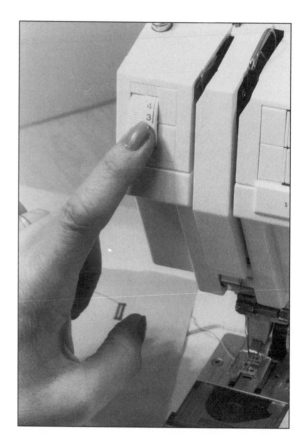

5. The pictured buttonhole was embellished with a decorative stitch. Engage the single pattern control key if your sewing machine offers this feature.

6. Test a variety of stitches combined with the standard buttonhole. Make notes of the pattern numbers and settings used on the practice sample. This increases buttonhole options while building your sewing machine skill.

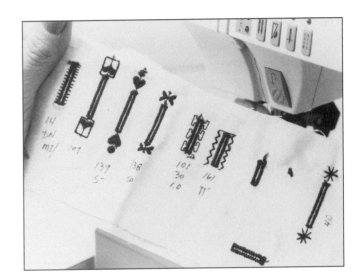

1. Sew buttons by machine for a fast and strong application. Check your manual for the correct presser foot, and to see if lowering the feed dogs is required. Many computerized machines have built-in programs for this purpose. Using a basic zigzag, select a stitch width from 3 mm–4.5 mm that will swing from hole to hole. Begin anchoring the button in place with straight stitches in the left hole. Zigzag swinging to the right hole. Turn the fly wheel by hand to test the swing, and repeat with the correct setting at least four times. Anchor the stitching with a straight stitch worked in the right hole of the button. To add play for fabric thickness, lay a used sewing machine needle between the holes to act as a spacer.

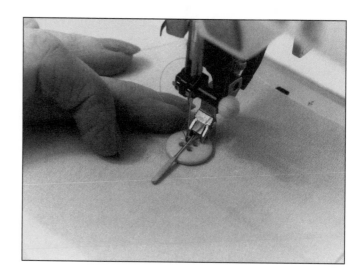

2. The needle will be encased in the stitches.

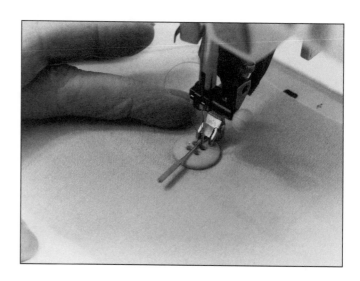

3. Repeat the procedure a second time for button with four holes. Slide the needle out when the stitching is complete.

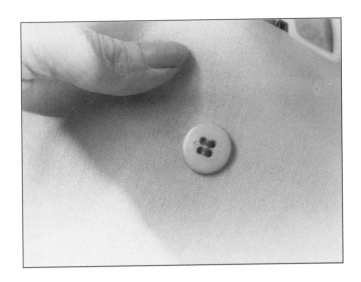

4. Use this method to attach individual sequins and embellishments. Nylon monofilament thread creates an invisible application, and is a strong and flexible attachment of found objects to cloth. The miniature sewing tools in the photo were secured in this manner.

1. With all line embroidery, use a presser foot that is grooved on the wrong side to allow satin stitches to feed easily. Select an embroidery needle with an oversized eye to avoid thread breakage.

2. Decorative stitches must be supported with a stabilizer. The product shown is excellent for creating a highly starched cloth that eliminates tearing off the stabilizer. Brush the product on the cloth and allow the suggested drying time. The resulting cloth will be extremely stiff, and the product will wash away with the first laundering.

3. Ask your dealer if an attachment is available for your model for circular embroidery. The accessory resembles a ruler with a covered pin on one end. For doing circular embroidery without an attachment, tape a thumbtack, with the point up, to the bed of your sewing machine. Push the fabric, with the right side facing up, through the thumb tack. Cover the point with a small cork to protect your hands. The distance from the tack to the needle is the radius of your circle.

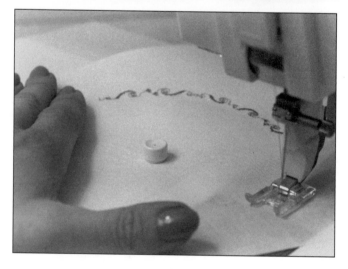

4. With the feed dogs raised, the machine will stitch in a circular path guided by the securing pin. Select one or combine several embroidery stitches for this technique.

SEQUENCE 11—CLEANING AND OILING THE MACHINE

1. Your machine should be oiled for every eight hours of sewing time. Clean the machine more frequently when the fabric or threads create excessive lint. You will need isopropyl alcohol, sewing machine oil, a small brush, and a cotton swab. Vacuum attachments are inexpensive and readily available for a thorough cleaning.

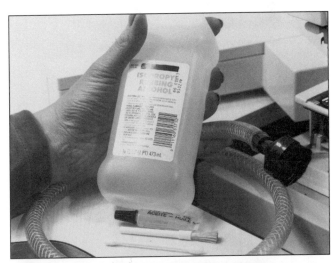

2. Remove the needle, presser foot, and the throat plate of your sewing machine.

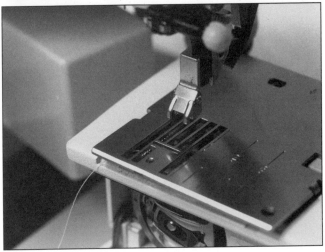

3. Brush the lint out of the feed dogs. A makeup brush works excellently for this task.

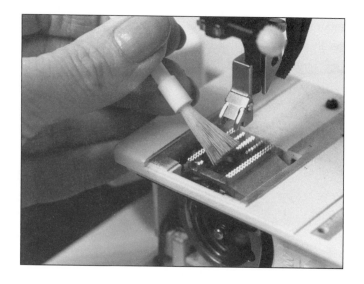

4. Canned air is recommended for blowing lint out of the bobbin area of the machine. DO NOT BLOW INTO THE MACHINE WITH YOUR MOUTH. THE MOISTURE IN YOUR BREATH CAN RUST THE METAL PARTS OF THE MACHINE.

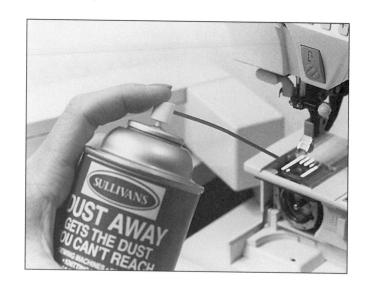

5. Turn the fly wheel of the machine and observe the machine's hook rotating or oscillating within a metal track. This track is commonly called the race. After removing the bobbin case, use a small brush to clean the race of your machine.

6. A soft cloth can be useful in removing excess oil and dirt.

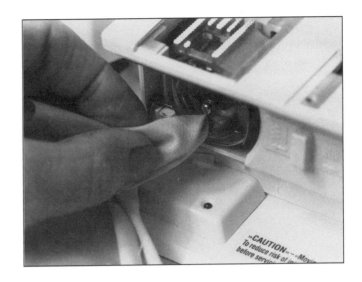

7. Dip a cotton swab in alcohol.

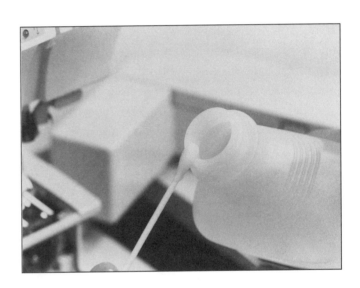

8. Clean away excess oil and dirt from the bobbin case.

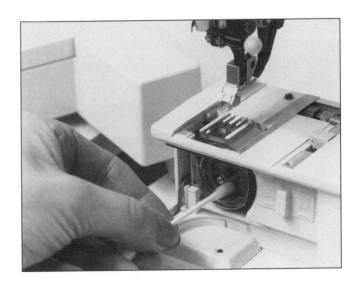

9. The collected dirt, if not removed, will build up and affect the machine's performance.

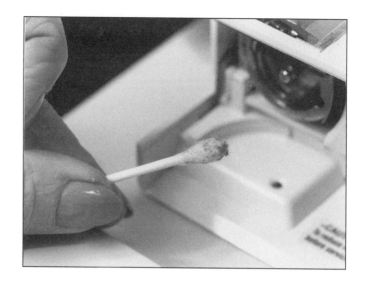

10. Check your machine manual to see if oiling is recommended. Many newer model machines are made of oil-impregnated metal, and additional oiling is not suggested. If your manual does suggest oiling, put a drop of oil on the race or hook of the machine. Without frequent oiling, the race will seize.

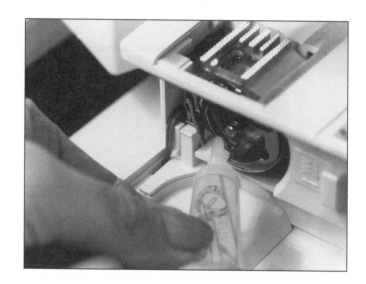

11. As you turn the wheel observe moving parts where metal joins metal. A drop of oil at the junctions will make the machine operate quietly. Follow oiling charts in your manual. Though oiling may be unnecessary for some models, frequent cleaning is important for all.

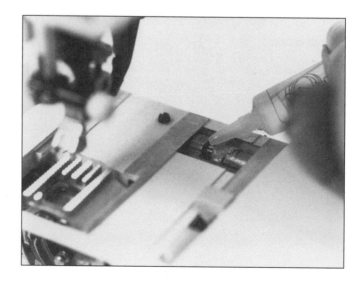

1. To insert decorative cord into a seam, a bias strip must be attached to one side of the cord. Use the blindstitch for this technique. This stitch is formed, on most sewing machines, with the straight stitches sewn to the needle right, and the zigzag swinging to the left of the needle. For this operation it will be most convenient to have the cord to the right of the needle, with the bias strip positioned to the needle left. The straight stitch, therefore, should be sewn to the needle left as well. If your machine has a mirror-image adjustment, select this option. The machine will now position the straight stitches on the bias, with the zigzag swinging over to the cording. Adjust the needle tension to a lighter setting, and the zigzag swing to its full width. The cording/bias assembly will lay flat due to more slack in the needle tension.

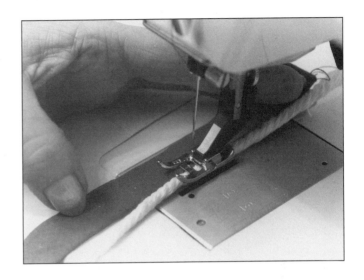

2. The straight stitch is made along the top edge of the bias fold line, with the zigzag attaching the cord to the strip.

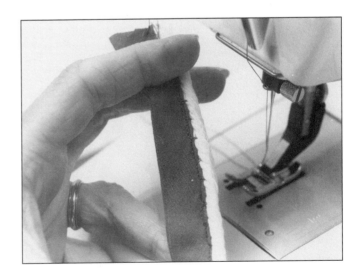

3. Sew the cord to one edge of the seam allowance before completing the seam. After construction, the cord will be firmly yet inconspicuously attached within the seam.

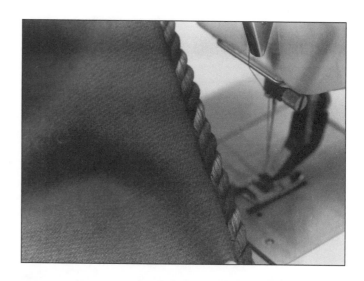

SEQUENCE 13—COUCHING

1. Many sewing machines, like New Home's Memory Craft 8000 pictured, have decorative stitches appropriate for couching multiple cords simultaneously.

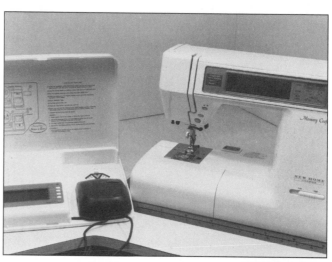

2. The pictured stitch is frequently used for topstitching.

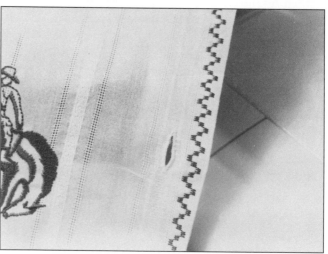

3. The stitch shown here is made of three separate rows of satin stitches in a step formation that uses the entire field of the sewing width. The decorative potential is to secure three separate ribbons or heavy threads on the surface of the fabric.

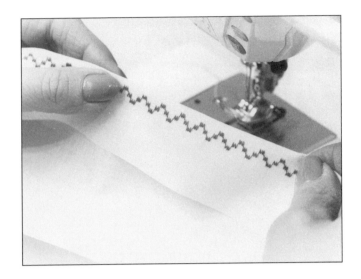

4. New Home, Elna, Singer, and Pfaff have presser feet that allow multiple cords to feed through the front of the foot during stitching. The foot prevents the cords intertwining. These feet are all snap-on low shank accessories. Check your dealer to see if one of these will accommodate your model.

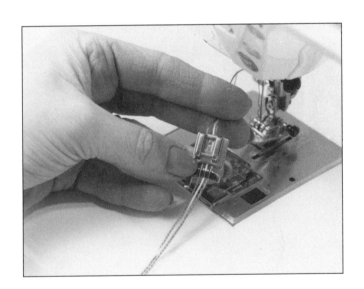

5. Insert cording into the foot and the stitches couch the cords. Pearl Crown rayon was used for the sample shown, but many threads are applicable. Silk ribbon, yarns, and Ribbon Floss will all work well.

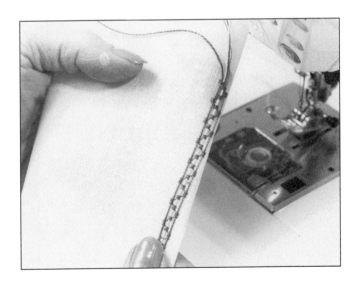

6. Most machines feature a three-step zigzag stitch commonly used for applying elastic.

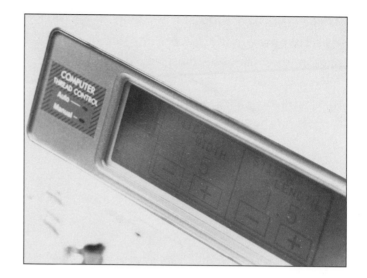

7. Using the triple cording foot, the elastic stitch usually delegated for utility work is transformed into a decorative treatment.

8. A simple yet effective cording can be accomplished with a straight stitch. Take a heavy yarn or cord and fold it in half. Secure the fold to the fabric surface with one stitch, and bring two equal lengths to either side of the needle.

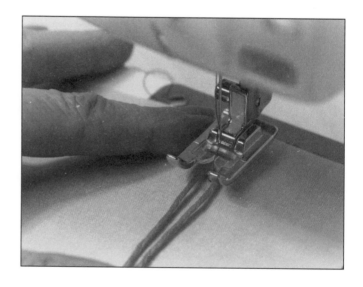

9. Cross the ends in front of the needle, and take one stitch.

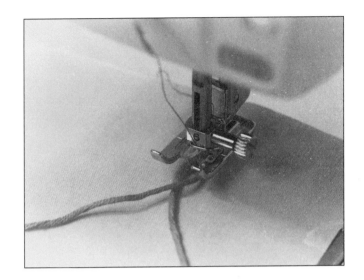

10. Repeat this procedure crisscrossing the yarn in front of the needle.

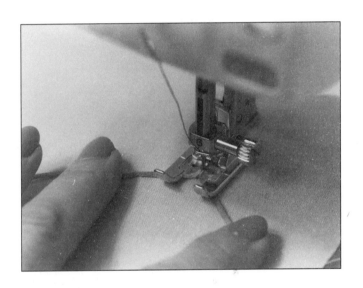

11. A couched braid will be formed on the surface of the cloth. As in all decorative work, it is necessary to stabilize the cloth to support the heavy surface yarns.

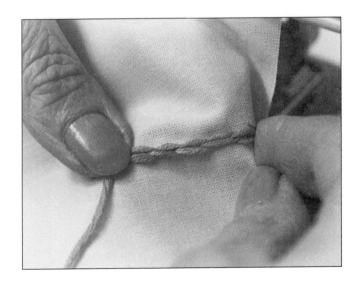

12. Textural variation can be added by alternating heavy yarns and ribbons.

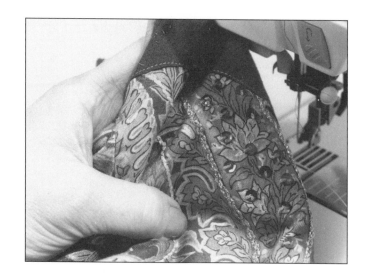

13. You can experiment with presser feet and apply them to multiple purposes. Hemmer feet are designed to turn a rolled hem, and are available in various sizes for use with a range of fabric weights. The scroll formation of the foot works well for applying heavy yarn.

14. Set the machine for a narrow-width zigzag and couch the yarn as it feeds through the foot scroll. The foot provides great control while couching.

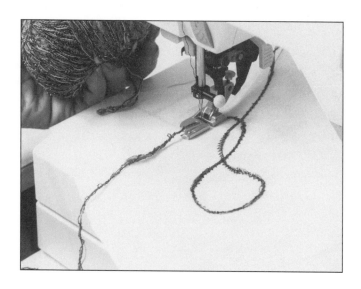

15. Silk ribbon and ultra suede strips have been couched to the surface of the garment pictured using a wide zigzag stitch. The sequin/ribbon foot used to attach the embellishments featured is a "Creative Foot" and is available to fit most machine models. Stabilizing the fabric is recommended for all couching.

SEQUENCE 14—CROSS-STITCHING

1. Many sewing machines today offer cross-stitches. The Pfaff 7550 pictured provided the greatest selection of line embroidery stitches. The cross-stitches can be adjusted by length and width to work within any evenweave cloth.

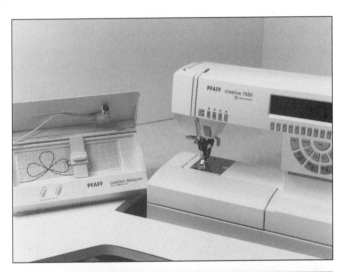

2. Cross-stitches shown vary from single to elaborate border patterns. The stitch on the right is a hemstitch accomplished with a wing needle. This was worked before the cross-stitches were embroidered on the tablecloth.

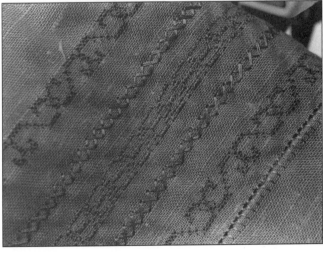

3. Use the quilting bar to ensure even rows of cross-stitching. Align the bar with the hem or folded edge of the cloth when beginning.

4. When approaching a corner, select the single pattern key, if your machine offers this feature. This control completes a full pattern and stops the machine. Complete the pattern, raise the presser foot with the needle in the fabric, and pivot your work.

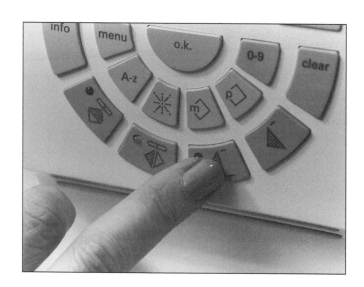

5. The corners should start and stop with a completed stitch. Remember to ensure the best stitch formation by stabilizing the cloth.

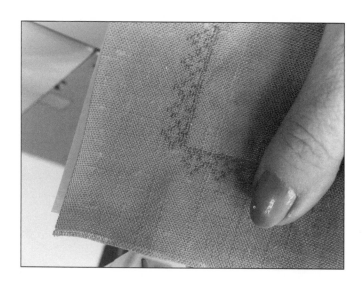

1. Draw the design on the right side of the fashion fabric, using a wash out or air-dry marker.

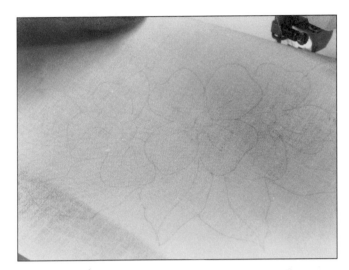

2. Set your machine for a medium-width satin stitch with the feed dogs raised. Stitch on the marked lines as shown, pivoting frequently to maintain sharp curves.

3. Use a water dissolvable stabilizer for this technique. You may use one layer on the wrong side of the fabric, or steam press two to three layers of the stabilizer together if more support is needed.

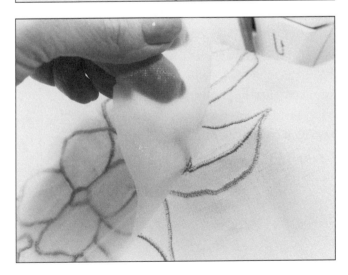

4. Cut the fabric layer out from within a design section, using a small sharp scissors.

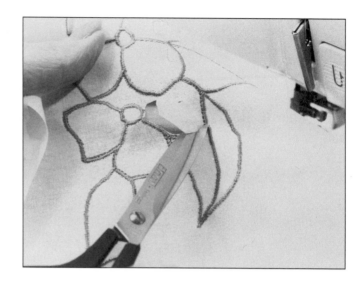

5. Leave the water dissolvable stabilizer behind the area to support additional stitchery.

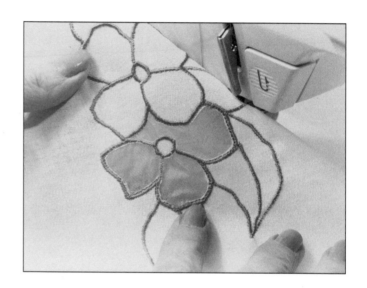

6. The collar shown has satin stitch or Richelieu bars. Some sections are backed with tulle. The Richelieu was added once the fabric was cut away, maintaining the stabilizer for support. The tulle can be inserted between the cloth and the stabilizer. Cut away the cloth after satin stitching, and trim the tulle to the opening size on the back.

7. This detail of the yellow jacket featured in color plate 3 shows cutwork unconventionally used. Flowers cut from decorator chintz fabric were appliquéd to the garment. Selected areas of the jacket had lamé positioned under the top layer. After outlining with satin stitching, the top layer was removed, revealing the accent lamé.

8. The yoke of this jacket was made using synthetic leather. The floral design was drawn on a fusible web and applied to the wrong side of the leather. Interior lines were cut away with a small scissors, and the completed yoke ironed to the jacket front using a press cloth. A buttonhole stitch was used to accent and add strength to the cut out sections. Traditional cutwork offers elegance, but the technique is appropriate for many fabrics and fashion treatments.

1. Machine darning is used to repair cut or worn garments. Cut the patch larger than the tear.

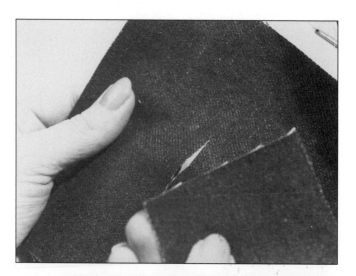

2. The patch may be applied using a fusible web and pressed in place. The patch may be applied to the right or wrong side of the tear.

3. Use an overlock stitch and sew the raw edge of the patch to the background fabric. Use a stabilizer on the wrong side if the background fabric is lightweight. The sample photographed was applied to the right side of the fabric with the patch placed over the tear. The patch was applied with the Viking #1 machine, which features a darning stitch formed with a sideways sewing motion. Beginning with the top edge, the machine sews the patch working from left to right. When the first side is completed, push a button and the machine sews the patch down its right edge. With another touch, the machine sews the lower edge of the patch. The final sewing sequence completes the left side working in reverse. The cloth does not need to be moved throughout the stitching sequence. This is a wonderful example of what a computerized sewing machine can offer for the home sewer.

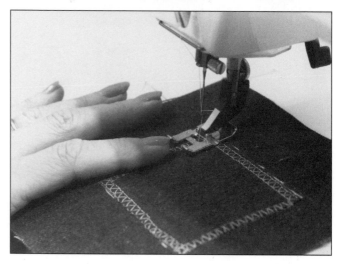

PLATE 1. White and Red wool Jacket. Jacket made and designed by the author on the Pfaff 7550. The design features pintucking and scallops made using a 2.5 mm double needle.

PLATE 2. Tweed Jacket Featuring Leather Cutwork Yoke. Made and designed by the author using Viking #1.

PLATE 3. Yellow Bolero Jacket featuring Large Floral Cutwork. Made and designed by the author using Singer Quantum XL-100.

PLATE 4. Appliquéd Castle Scene worked on sweatshirt. Made and designed by Kathy Davis of Lake Ronkonkoma, New York, on the Brother Pacesetter 7000.

PLATE 5. Denim Jacket featuring embellished yoke. Made and designed by the author on New Home's Memory Craft 8000 using free-motion embroidery.

PLATE 6. Winter Scene Jacket worked on sweatshirt backing. Made and designed by Kathy Davis of Lake Ronkonkoma, New York. The embroidery utilizes the Moskowitz design card on the Brother Pacesetter 7000 sewing machine.

PLATE 7. Pink and Black Two-Piece Linen Dress. Made and designed by the author on Pfaff 7550. Black linen was worked with one 40 mm stitch to create embroidered fabric. Double piping was used in all the seams.

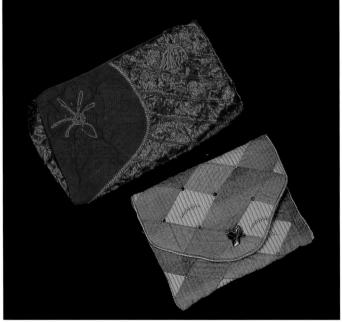

PLATE 8. Two purses. Made and designed by the author using the Pfaff 7550. Red purse has trapunto accents; the other purse was embroidered using a single pattern repeat.

PLATE 9. Sewing Machine. Made and designed by the author using the Pfaff 7550 machine. Appliquéd and embellished.

PLATE 10. Towels. Made by author using the Brother Pacesetter machine, the Singer Quantum XL-100, and the Baby Lock Esante.

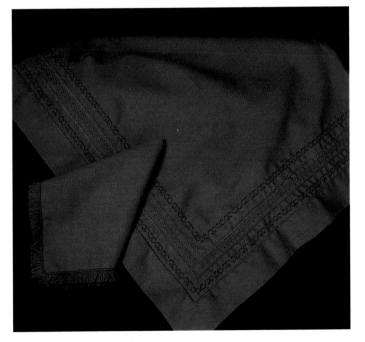

PLATE 11. Tablecloth. Made by the author using the Pfaff 7550 featuring cross-stitch patterns and hemstitching.

PLATE 12. Smocked Dresses. Made by the author. The navy and pink stripe dress was made on the Baby Lock Esante and the light blue dress was made on the Pfaff 7550 machine.

PLATE 13. Egyptian-Style Vest. Made and designed by Toby Davidson of Coram, New York. The vest was strip-pieced and features couching made on the Bernina 1130.

PLATE 14. Crazy Quilt Vest. Made and designed by Toby Davidson of Coram, New York. The vest was couched and embellished with the Bernina 1130 machine.

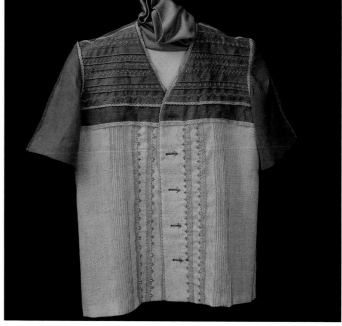

PLATE 15. Black/Silver/Maroon Vest. Made and designed by Toby Davidson of Coram, New York. Embroidery was done using the Bernina 1130 machine.

PLATE 16. Taupe/Natural Linen Blouse. Made and designed by the author. Blouse features pintucking and heirloom stitching using the Pfaff 7550 machine.

PLATE 17. Pink/Gray/Print Vest. Made and designed by the author. Vest features embellishment, ultra suede appliqué, couching, and double piping. Made on the Pfaff 7550.

PLATE 18. Black and Gold Bolero Jacket. Made and designed by the author on the Pfaff 1475 CD machine.

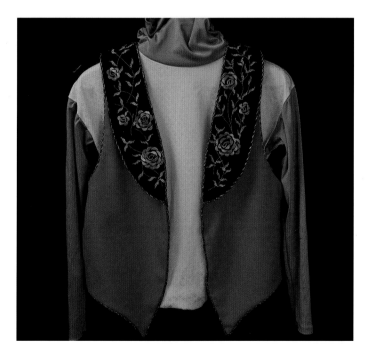

Plate 19. Maroon Vest with Black Embellished Lapels. Made and designed by the author on the Elna Diva machine.

PLATE 20. Natural-Colored Vest Embellished With Appliqué Flowers. Made and designed by the author on the Pfaff 1475 CD machine.

PLATE 21. Purple Velvet Vest Embellished with Gold Thread Embroidery. Made on the Pfaff 1475 CD machine using bobbin embroidery for gold grid lines and a repeated single pattern worked at all the intersection lines.

PLATE 22. Gray Velvet Vest with Ribbon Pleats. Made and designed by the author using Viking #1 machine. Yoke features bobbin embroidery.

PLATE 23. Western Shirt. Made by author using the New Home Memory Craft 8000. Purchased white shirt with added yoke, cuff, and collar, and embroidery added by author.

PLATE 24. Blue Dress featuring Cutwork. Made by the author on the Pfaff 1475 CD machine.

PLATE 25. Lingerie Set. Made by the author using the Brother Pacesetter 7500 machine.

PLATE 26. Fan Dress. Made and designed by the author. The dress is machine quilted and embellished using the Bernina 1230 machine.

PLATE 27. Joanie's Dolls. All the dolls were made and designed by Joan Ziccardy of Long Island, New York. The dolls and their clothing were made and embellished using a Pfaff 1475 CD machine.

PLATE 28. Christmas Quilt. Made and designed by Kathy Davis of Lake Ronkonkoma, New York. The lettering and embroidery were worked on the Brother Pacesetter 7000.

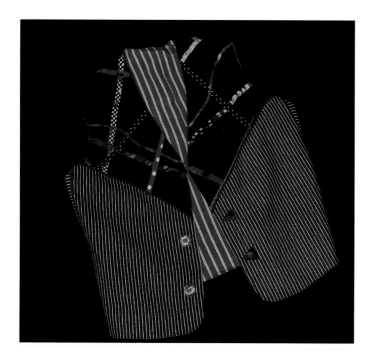

PLATE 29. NAVY Stripe Vest featuring Strip Quilted Yoke. Made and designed by the author. The jacket features couched sequins and embellished piping using the Brother Pacesetter 7500.

PLATE 30. Baltimore Anew Queen-Size Quilt. Made by the author. Embroidery, appliqué, and quilting done on Pfaff 1475 CD machine.

1. Full service sewing machines may offer an additional embroidery bed for hooped embroidery. A library of design cards is available to upgrade built-in embroidery programs.

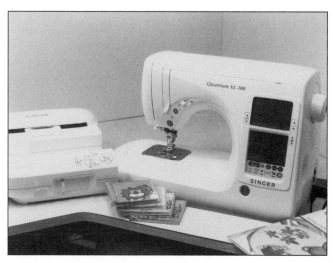

2. The designs are stitched in multicolored or single color segments. The machine pauses after a color is completed and signals the operator to change thread. Embroidery is controlled by a power button, rather than a foot control. The machine runs on its own, freeing the operator from sitting with foot to pedal for long periods.

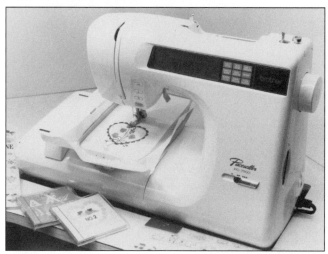

3. Creativity is achieved by the addition of a scanner. This accessory allows the sewer to trace or draw an original design that is recorded on an embroidery card. This card is then sewed out by the embroidery machine.

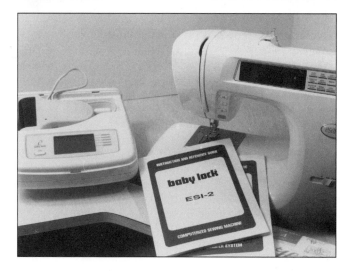

4. Most embroidery today is sewn using rayon and metallic threads. The thread has great sheen and is available in an endless color assortment. The thread is fragile at times and prone to breakage. Use a top-stitching or embroidery needle to avoid this problem. Select a presser foot that allows optimum visibility like the clear foot shown.

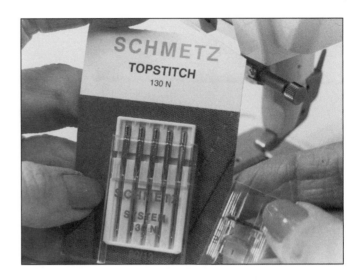

5. Always stabilize the cloth for embroidery.

6. For line embroidery, use the quilting bar on your machine to set up parallel rows of stitches.

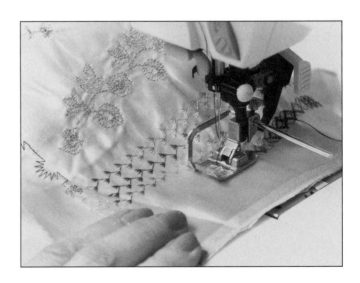

7. Combine patterns to create new borders and motifs.

8. Practice samples can be saved and later included in garments. The Embroidered fabric shown in this photograph was cut to form the yoke of the garment. The quilting bar maintained even rows that were acceptable for garment construction. This is an example of a practical application for experimental exercises.

9. Satin-filled stitches from the machine's built-in memory, like the heart stitch shown in the photograph, are splendid for appliqué.

10. Embellish appliqué scenes with textured stitchery. Remember to use the button application method to attach three-dimensional details like the bicycle pictured.

11. The single pattern command on your sewing machine can be an embellishment aid. The purple vest shown in color plate 21 was accented with a single leaf at the intersection of gold stitches.

12. Equipped with an assortment of line embroidery stitches you can create large motifs by combining small elements.

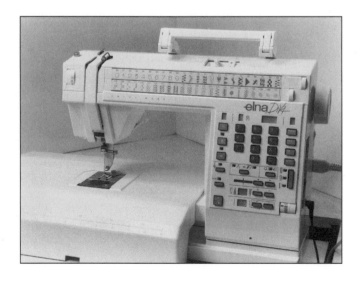

13. When embroidering a flower, start by sewing the stems. Work in the order that the flower grows: stem, leaves, and bud. Position the presser foot to sew from the stem out for leaf placement.

14. Begin creating the flower from the center of the bloom out. Offset two curved scallop stitches to make a center. Please note again, the background fabric is stabilized.

15. Select a scallop stitch that resembles a semicircle or petal for the second pass. Surround the flower center with four of these scallops.

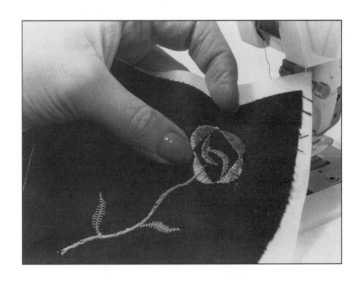

16. The petal scallop is repeated below the previous row to enlarge the bloom. Notice how closely the scallops must be positioned to maintain the flower's visual structure. Add scallops to one side, or surround the center in a circular direction for a flower with a frontal view.

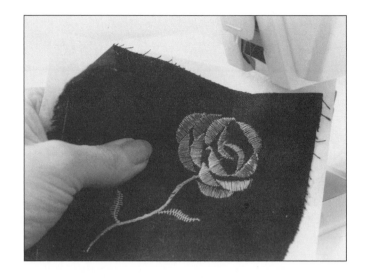

17. The lapels of the vest (shown in color plate 19) are embellished with roses. The cover photograph inspired the flowers that can be easily sewn with many sewing machines.

1. You can gently ease a seam to fit a smaller seam by adjusting your machine controls.

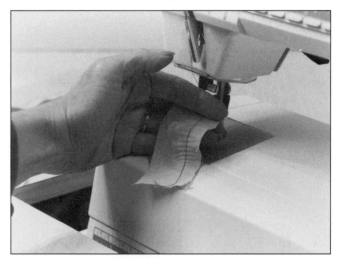

2. Increase the needle tension on your machine to draw the fabric up slightly.

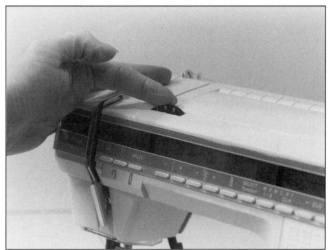

3. Decrease the stitch length to evenly distribute and control the puckering.

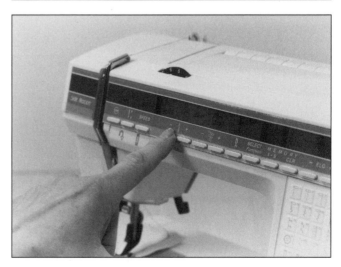

1. Select the three-step zigzag stitch for applying elastic. This stitch is formed of three straight stitches that work diagonally across the sewing path. This stitch does not sew through the elastic threads but across their weave, maintaining elasticity.

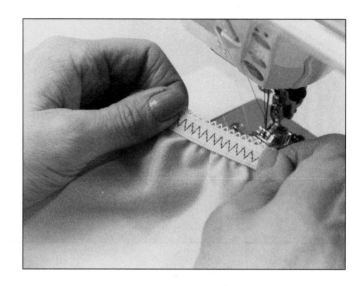

2. With the needle down in the work, stretch the elastic evenly, distributing the garment fullness to the cut size of the elastic. For additional control, engage the needle down option, if your machine offers this feature.

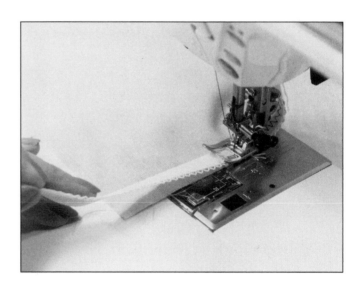

1. When making eyelets, drop or cover the feed dogs on your sewing machine.

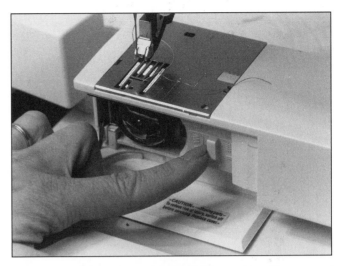

2. Many models provide accessory covers for the throat plate. Removal of the presser foot is usually necessary.

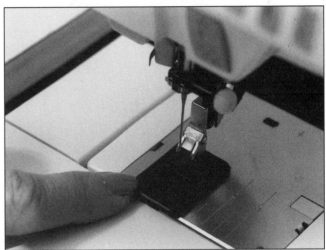

3. A small cut is made in the hooped fabric.

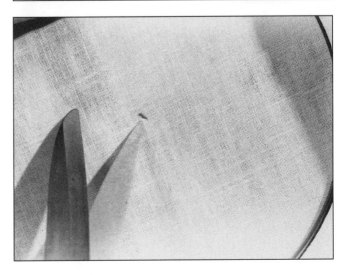

4. The throatplate cover usually has a rounded projection that surrounds the needle hole. Press the fabric opening over this rim.

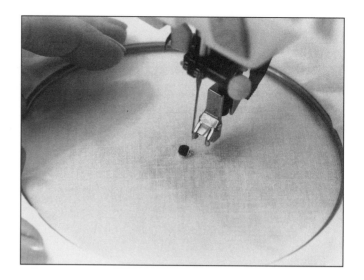

5. Use a medium-width satin stitch and sew manually, turning the hoop. Rotate the hoop several times, gradually building stitch layers to encase the hole.

6. The completed satin stich eyelet is shown in the photo. Experiment with additional decorative stitches for eyelet variations. Scallop stitches and floral patterns varying in width are most effective.

1. Fagoting is a "stitch bridge" decoratively connecting two fabrics. Frequently an underlayer of fabric or trim is included. Select a stitch that originates from the center needle position and swings equally to the sides.

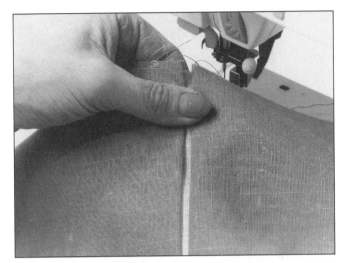

2. Determine the maximum opening the stitch needs in order to engage the folds. Baste the layers to maintain the opening size and to reduce fabric shift.

3. The stitch shown is a featherstitch. Explore additional stitch programs for this simple but effective construction detail.

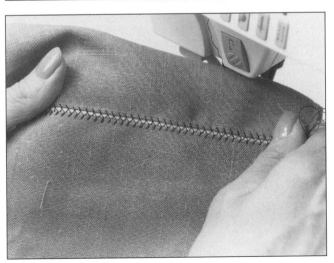

1. Flat fell seams are used on jeans and men's shirts. When sewing denim, use jeans needles. A felling foot, pictured, is helpful for this procedure. The Jean-a-ma-jig™ is a notion that allows the presser foot to feed easily over thick seams.

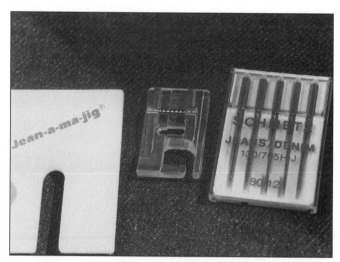

2. The seam is sewn with the wrong sides together. Trim one edge of the sewn seam to ¼".

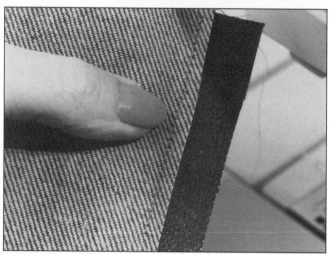

3. Fold the larger seam over the trimmed side, bringing its raw edge even with the seamline. The felling presser foot holds the fold as you sew. The foot opening is a convenient guide for maintaining an even rolled seam.

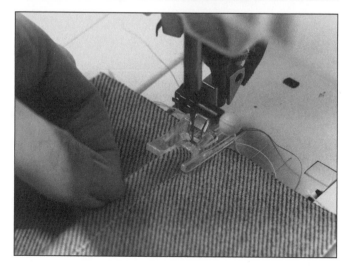

4. Curved seams like the armseye seams are problematical for this traditional construction. Sew the seams with right sides facing each other, as in normal construction. Trim to ¼" seam allowance and overlock the raw edges for a clean finish. Press the seams toward the garment body. On the right side, topstitch ¼" from the seam for a mock flat fell seam.

5. For heavy denim seams, position the Jean-a-ma-jig behind the back of the presser foot. This elevates the presser foot back to the same height as in the front. The machine is then able to feed the cloth without problems.

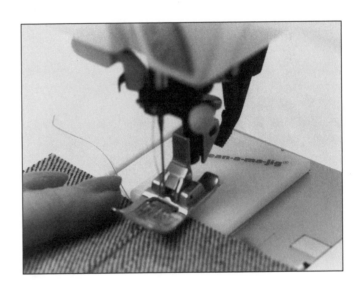

1. "Free motion" implies that the operator will control the feed of the fabric when sewing. The feed dogs are dropped or covered during this procedure. Use a darning foot (available for most models), the Big Foot™, a generic product, or a spring needle shown below the two feet. The spring needle fits all home sewing machines and can serve as a substitute for a darning foot. These attachments allow for freedom of motion and maximum visibility. Set your stabilized cloth in a hoop for this embroidery.

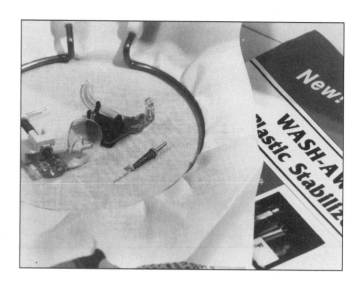

2. Begin by outlining the design. Fill areas with a straight stitch or narrow zigzag. The operator is free to move the cloth in all directions. Naturally, practice is essential to build your eye-hand coordination for even control.

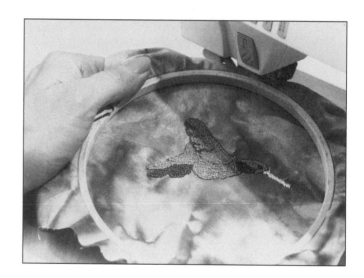

1. Fringing is a common edge finish for open weave fabrics. A row of stitching is placed evenly around all the edges. The quilting bar is helpful in sewing an even edge.

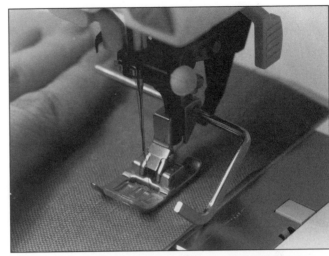

2. The stitch shown is a hem stitch commonly used on linens and in heirloom sewing. The weave of the fabric is opened when this stitch is worked with a wing needle. After stitching, remove the threads from the border.

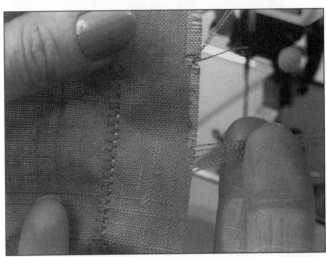

3. The completed edge is attractive and will withstand laundering.

1. The fringe presser foot has a blade in the center of the foot as shown. Set the machine to a zigzag stitch with a width of 3 mm and a short stitch length. The zigzag will form over the blade of the presser foot.

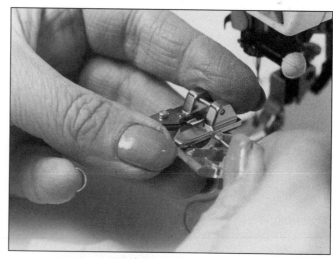

2. Start by marking a circle on your fabric. Remember to stabilize the fabric.

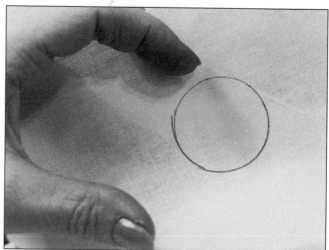

3. Stitch on the drawn lines, pivoting the needle frequently to maintain the curve.

4. Continue to sew in circles, in progressively narrowing turns filling the circle with stitches. Keep the turns smooth by raising the presser foot frequently and pivoting.

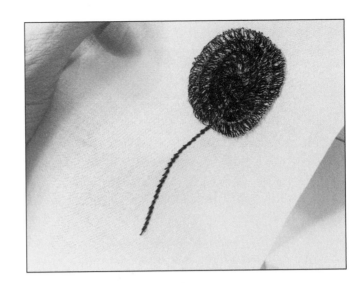

5. Fringing can be an effective embellishment for joining two folded edges.

6. When stitching is completed, spread the seam open to create a fagoted seam. Maintain the separation by attaching this seam to further construction, or fusing a layer of cloth behind the seam.

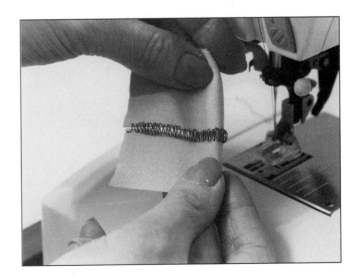

1. There are a variety of methods to gather fabric. One way is to position your finger behind the cloth as you sew to impede the feed of the fabric. A gentle gather results that is frequently sufficient to ease sleeve caps. The most common method of gathering short sections of fabric is to adjust the stitch length to a long setting of 6 mm. Make two parallel rows of stitches within the seam allowance. Knot the needle threads and gently pull the bobbin threads. The fullness can be adjusted evenly before attaching the fabric to a seam.

2. Presser feet are available for gathering and ruffling material. The two smaller feet, both plastic and metal, are shirring or gathering feet. The large foot is a ruffler, and will create pleated and gathered fabric.

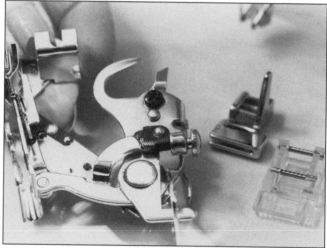

3. The fabric on the right was gathered with the shirring foot, while the material on the left shows the deep pleats the ruffler produces.

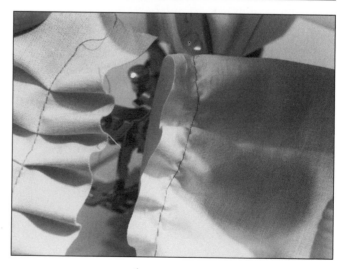

4. The gathering foot will create a sewed-in fullness that can be adjusted to a predetermined size. This presser foot is inexpensive but extremely useful.

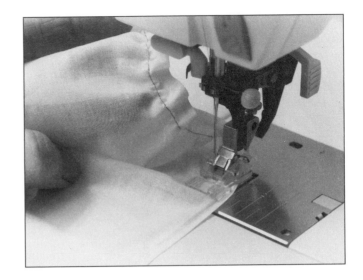

5. The gathering is effected by two machine settings, the stitch length and the needle tension. Increase the needle tension as shown in the photograph to a tight setting. With the foot in place, gather a sample of cloth. Increase the stitch length until the gathering is suitable.

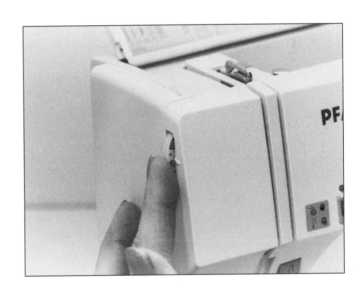

6. Rufflers have several controls. The front gauge is marked 1, 6, and 12. A star or zero may be marked as well. The numbers refer to the pleat frequency. Set the gauge at one and the attachment will create a pleat for every stitch. Set the number at six and a pleat will be formed every six stitches. Obviously the stitch length alters the ruffle: The shorter the stitch, the more frequent the pleat. When the gauge is set on the star or zero, pleating is stopped. This setting allows convenient attachment of additional fabric without removing the foot.

Besides screwing the foot to the presser foot bar, the fork on the right of the foot must be positioned over the needle screw. The foot causes considerable vibration as it works. Tighten the needle screw periodically to prevent the needle loosening.

A screw to the left side of the attachment controls the depth of the pleat. Loosen the screw to create a more gathered appearance.

Fabric placed between the blades of the ruffler is gathered or pleated. Material positioned under the foot is sewn only. With relative ease you may gather fabric and seam to a second layer of cloth in the same operation. This may also be accomplished with the smaller gathering feet. Cloth placed under the gathering feet, in direct contact with the feed dogs, is shirred. If the foot has a lip for the insertion of a second layer, this fabric will remain ungathered. Attachment and gathering can be quickly accomplished with both feet.

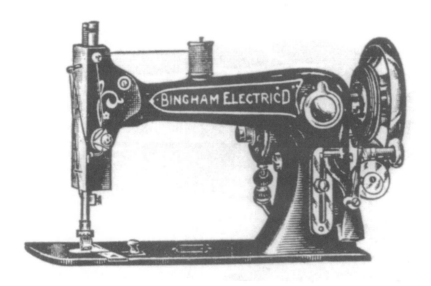

1. A hemstitch needle is a single wing needle for decorative openwork on tightly woven fabrics.

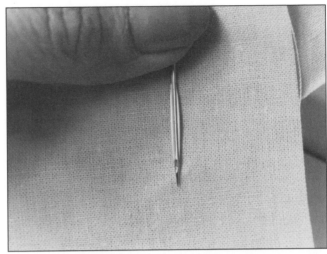

2. Stitch programs used for hemstitching have the needle repeatedly entering the same hole in the cloth. The needle, during this formation, spreads the cloth apart creating a decorative space or hole.

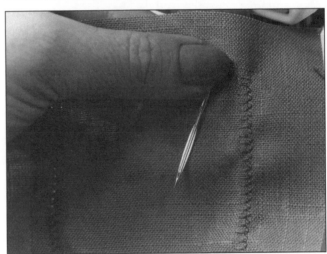

3. Stabilize the fabric with Perfect Sew™ for added support. Hemstitching can be combined with cross stitching or other decorative stitches. Make your own Swiss insertion as shown.

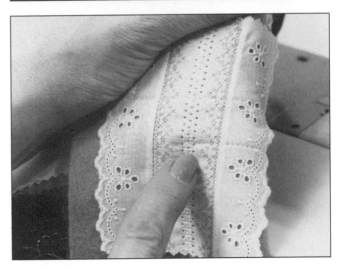

1. Free-motion embroidery or line embroidery stitched with the feed dogs raised can be used to create reembroidered lace. Support the foundation tulle or lace with several layers of wash-away stabilizer. Secure all the layers in a hoop. Position the hoop under the presser foot with feed dogs raised for line embroidery. For free-motion embroidery drop the feed dogs. When the embroidery is completed, remove the hoop, and tear away excess stabilizer. Wet the embroidery to dissolve the residue that may remain.

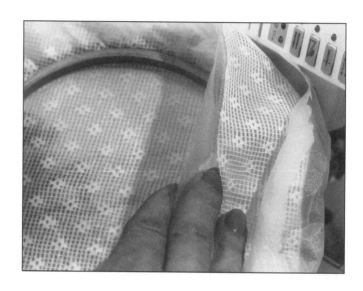

2. The lingerie insert shown was worked in the manner discussed in step 1 above. The floral spray was executed by Brother's Pacesetter 7500 embroidery machine using a design card. The scallops were stitched with the feed dogs raised. Excess fabric was trimmed away to form an edge.

1. Position the lace over the background fabric. Add a tear-away stabilizer under all the layers.

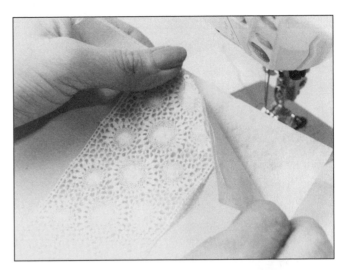

2. Use a narrow zigzag approximately 2.5 mm in length and width to attach the lace to the background fabric. The needle should swing into the lace border and enter the background fabric. Remove the stabilizer when the zigzag is completed.

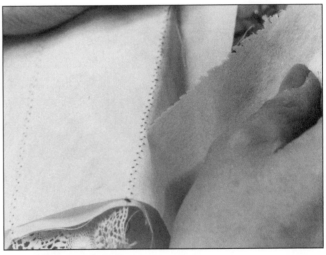

3. Cut away the background fabric leaving a narrow seam allowance. Finger press the seam allowance into the background area.

4. Straight stitch parallel to the lace border into the insertion seam allowance. This prevents the seams curling into the lace area, and reinforces the application.

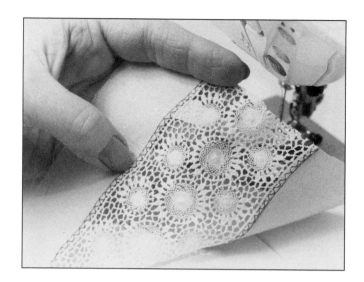

1. Real leather is an exciting accent material for pocket flaps, lapels, and yokes. Work with small areas at first to gain confidence for larger projects.

2. Leather needles have a slight cutting point for leather and heavy nonwoven synthetics. Presser feet with teflon coating along the bottom eliminate sticking. Teflon strips are available which can be applied to any presser foot. The right equipment turns a frequently difficult sewing problem into a routine sewing job.

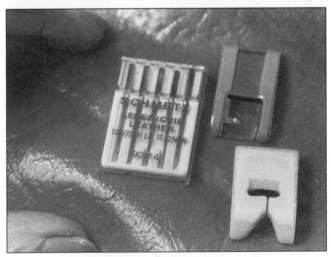

3. Ultrasuede featured on the vest in the photograph is different in composition from real leather. This fabric is not a leather product but a tightly knit polyester. Use a size 70 microtex needle for Ultrasuede.

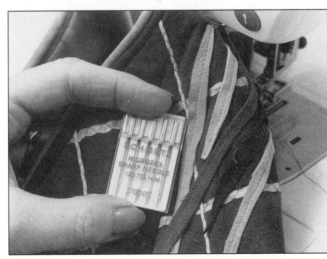

1. Computerized sewing machines like the Pfaff 7550 shown here offer lettering in a variety of styles and sizes. The machine's memory allows words to be saved and sewed out as you work or stored for future projects. A digitized scanner provides access to the machine's storage capacity. You may program new stitches and your own signature with the aid of this device.

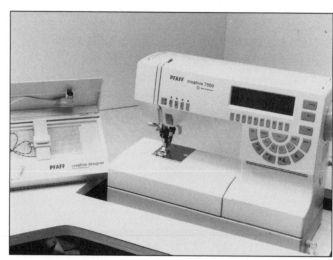

2. Combine decorative stitches with lettering.

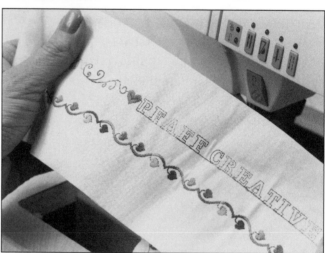

3. Machine models that offer alphabets provide full-size plastic sample sheets. Monogram placement is set by placing the stencil over the cloth. A hole shows where the needle will begin to stitch each letter. Mark the hole with a marker and place the needle at this point. Large motifs and lettering are printed on the placement stencils. The Brother Pacesetter overlay shown in this picture displays the placement used when planning a child's coveralls.

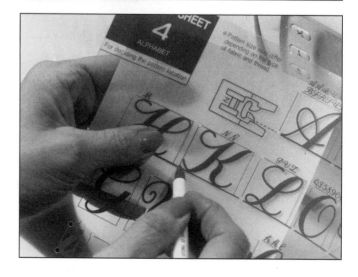

1. No single item affects the sewing performance of your machine more than the use of the correct needle. Always have a range of needles on hand. Change the needle frequently, and select the appropriate type and size for the job at hand.

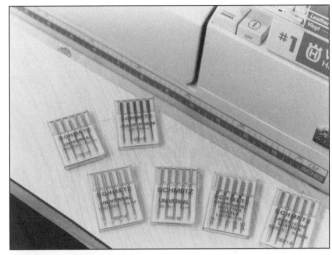

2. The flat part of the needle is placed away from the direction of the needle threading. Check the machine manual for specific threading instructions.

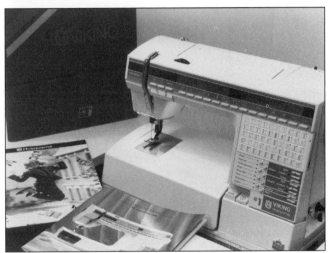

3. The needle type and sizes are marked on the needle case and on the top of the needle.

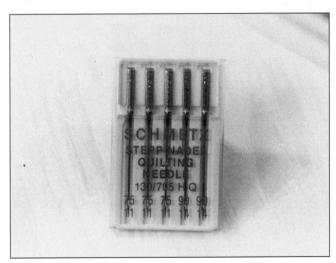

4. To view the needle markings, rotate the case 90 degrees. The top of the case will serve as a magnifier to allow the size to be easily read across the needle top.

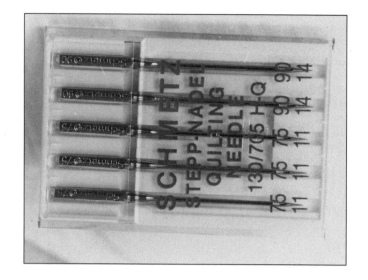

5. Double needles are available in a variety of sizes and types. The double hemstitch needle shown is available with one winged needle and one regular for decorative work.

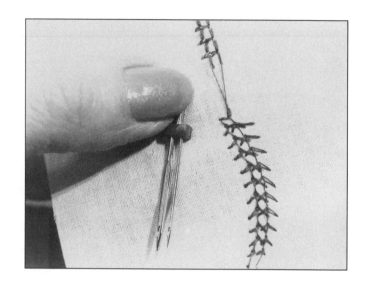

6. When sewing with a double needle, engage the twin needle key on your sewing machine if you have this feature. This will reduce the swing of the needle, preventing breakage.

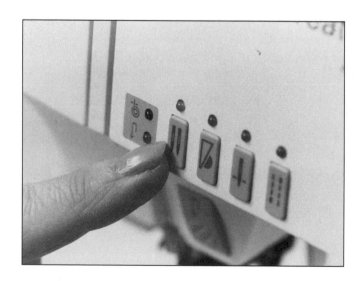

7. The stitch formation of the double hem-stitch needle shown is commonly used for heirloom sewing.

8. Triple needles employ three needles on a crossbar from a single shaft. Use a thread cone to hold the third spool of thread. The bobbin will form a zigzag on the wrong side of the cloth. Use similar weight thread for all the needle spools to ensure correct tension. The needle tension is regulated by two round metal disks, commonly called tension disks, that squeeze the thread with varying pressure. The pressure is set by the numbered dial on the front or side of your sewing machine. Pressure is applied only when the pressure foot is down. When the foot is raised the disks open, allowing the thread to be removed or replaced. Separate the thread layers with two on one side of the tension disk, and one apart.

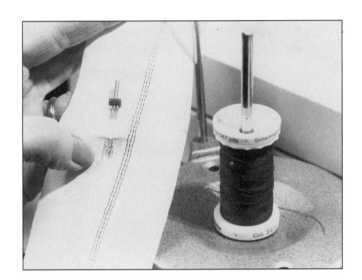

1. An overlock presser foot has a pin along the right side of the needle to support stitches that fall on the fabric edge.

2. Overlock stitching provides an excellent finish for knit seams to reduce bulk. Overlap the seams as shown, with the wrong side of one edge over the right side of the other.

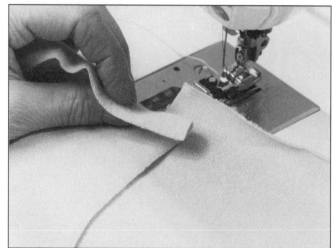

3. Trim away excess fabric from the seam edges.

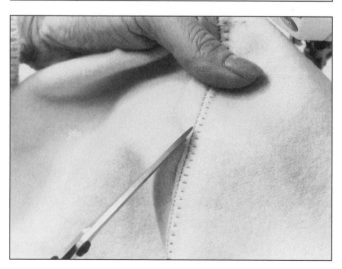

4. The resulting finish eliminates bulk and provides necessary flexibility. Many machines feature a variety of overlock stitches. A simple zigzag will be sufficient with a lightweight fabric. As the weight and weave change, the overlock formation alters. The overlock formation increases in width and length to maintain the integrity of the seam and the raw edge. Check the machine manual for the overlock stitch suitable for your fabric.

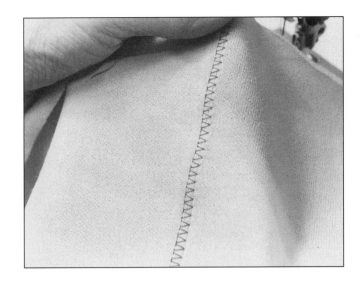

SEQUENCE 34—PINTUCKING

1. Pintucking can be accomplished with a zigzag sewing machine that has front threading. The equipment required is a double needle and a pintucking foot. The needles come in a variety of sizes and needle separation. If a pintucking foot is not available for your machine, generic feet can be used. You may substitute a foot that has a bottom grooved out to allow the passage of pleats.

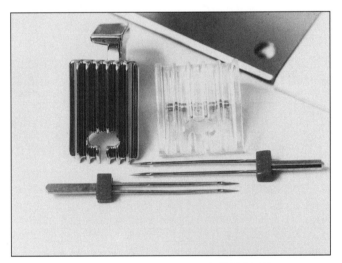

2. The pleats form under the groove of the foot as shown. Increase the needle tension to make the pleat more pronounced. Even rows are established by using the grooves or the outside edge of the foot for spacing.

3. A heavy thread or cording can be fed through the throat plate opening. Lay the thread to the back of the throat plate, and the cord will be caught inside the forming pleats.

4. Pfaff offers a blade that can be laid over the throat plate hole when pintucking. This helps to make the pleats more pronounced without adding a filler cord.

5. For heirloom sewing, space the pintucks the width of the foot. Return to fill the spaces with decorative stitches. The pleats will be convenient sewing guides. The stitches featured are sewn with a wing needle using the Pfaff built-in embroidery stitches.

6. Rows of pintucks are beautiful additions to the front of any garment. Cut the sections from your pattern a few inches larger. Pintuck an oversized cut of fabric, then overlay the pattern for a finished cut of the garment.

7. Pintucking removes fullness. This is a great functional and attractive method of easing a sleeve into an armseye, or as a dart replacement for a skirt front.

1. Piping is made by sewing a strip over a filling of cord. If the piping is to be used in a curved seam, the strip should be cut on the bias of woven cloth or crossgrain of a knit. When inserted in a straight seam, the strip need not be bias. The piping is commonly cut 1½" in width, but this can vary to fit the thickness of the filler cord used.

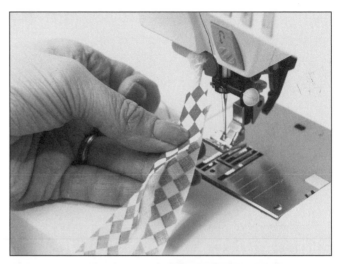

2. Use your sewing machine zipper foot. An alternate foot is a bulky piping, knit edge, or pearl foot. These feet have a deep trough in the bottom that will allow for carrying the cording. Move the needle position, if your machine has this capability, close to the cord as you stitch.

3. Double piping is easily built on the basic piping unit. Center the second strip over the previous seamline, and sew it in place with raw edges aligned.

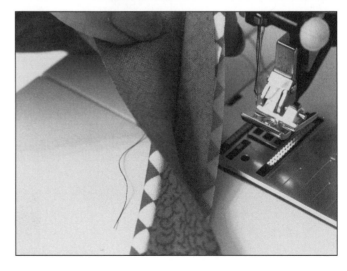

4. Insert the cord into the second strip, and stitch again.

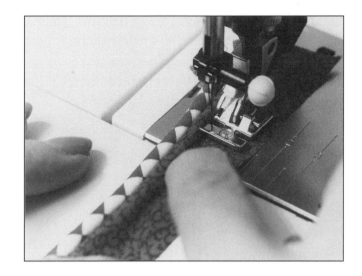

5. The completed double piping can be added to your project as you see fit. Lighten the filler weight for insertion in construction seams of lightweight fabric. Double piping does have a definite right and wrong side. Remember to put the finished side, as shown, to the right side of the fabric when inserting it into a seam.

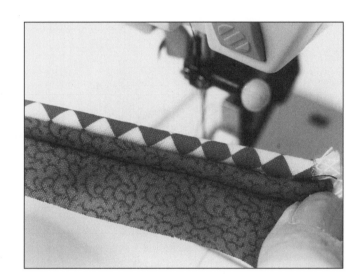

6. Inexpensive commercial piping can be embellished by the addition of decorative stitching. Load the needle and the bobbin with the same thread for a reversible trim. The piping shown is enhanced with a buttonhole or pin stitch using metallic thread.

7. Experiment with stitches for creating embellished piping. Adjust the stitch width to keep the needle on the cording. Use the presser foot appropriate for satin stitching. You may need to help the feed by gently guiding the piping from the back with your hands as you sew. Pfaff owners should engage the dual feed to draw the piping as they stitch.

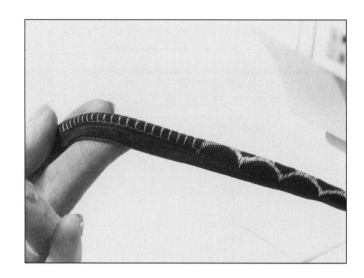

SEQUENCE 36—QUILTING

1. The movement of the cloth by the sewing machine can result in shift between the layers. The presser foot pushes against the top layer of cloth a bit faster than the feed dogs move the lower layer. This movement is exaggerated with a filling of batting. To solve this problem, use an evenfeed or walking foot. Many Pfaff sewing machines have a built-in dual feed system. This is engaged by pulling the black arm behind the presser foot. This mechanism eliminates all shifting between the layers. If you can manually adjust the foot pressure, reduce this setting to minimize shift.

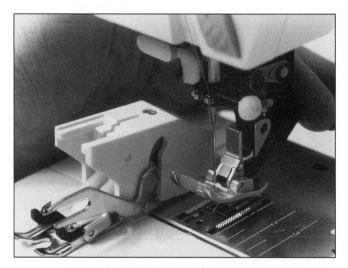

2. The center presser foot is a quilting foot by Elna that measures a one-quarter inch seam. Many manufacturers offer an accessory foot for this purpose. You may move the needle position of your machine to achieve a ¼" seam allowance. The Big Foot on the left is a generic darning foot made by an independent company to fit most low shank machines. It features a mushroom-like needle opening. This foot

provides excellent visibility and a convenient stitching reference. Use machine quilting needles for the best stitch formation.

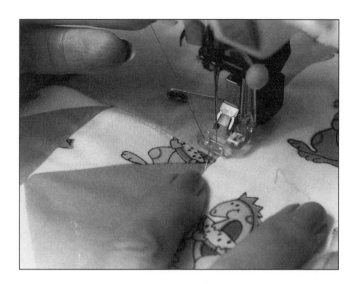

3. Begin your quilting by manually turning the machine wheel and raising the bobbin thread through the layers of the machine to the top. Always turn the wheel of your machine toward you. This action is most easily accomplished with the presser foot lever in a raised position.

4. Drop the presser foot, and take several stitches in the same hole to secure the thread. Clip the tails and quilt. The presser foot shown is a darning foot for free-motion quilting. The feed dogs should be lowered for this procedure. Notice the quilt is secured with safety pins. Do not thread-baste machine quilting. Using size 1 or smaller safety pins, pin the layers together at 4" intervals. Position the pins out of your sewing path to eliminate removal as you work.

5. As machine quilting has increased in popularity, new methods have developed. An effective quilting stitch can be worked that mocks the appearance of a running stitch with spaces between stitches. Use a nylon monofilament thread or thread matching the fabric color in the needle. Fill the bobbin with the thread color of the quilting stitches. Set the machine for a triple action stretch stitch. This is a stitch that moves forward, back once, then advances twice. Increase the needle tension to a high setting, a number 8 or 9.

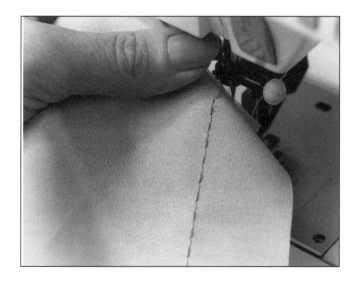

The resulting stitch is formed when the increased needle tension draws the bobbin thread to the surface of the cloth.

6. The pattern shown for this type quilting was modeled on Japanese Sashiko needlework.

SEQUENCE 37—ROLLED HEMS

1. Rolled-hem feet are available in a variety of widths, as shown, to accommodate different weight fabrics.

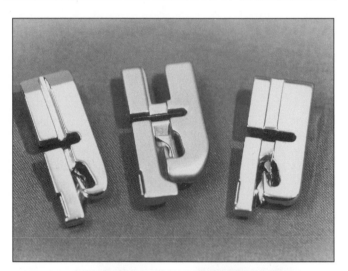

2. Begin the hem by rolling an inch along the raw edge of the fabric. Starch the fabric for ease in handling.

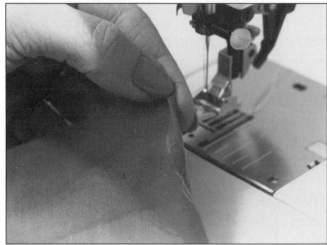

3. Stitch the first inch under the foot, then bring the fold up into the scroll.

4. Maintain a firm tension on the fabric so you can feed it evenly into the scroll.

5. Complete the hem along one side to end. If needed, repeat the adjacent side in the same manner, overlapping the ends as shown.

1. Use an overlock foot, or a foot used for a blind hem for this procedure. Generic feet, pictured on the left, are available to fit most models for satin-edge stitching. The foot has a pin to the right of the needle to support the fabric as the machine applies a dense satin stitch along the fabric edge.

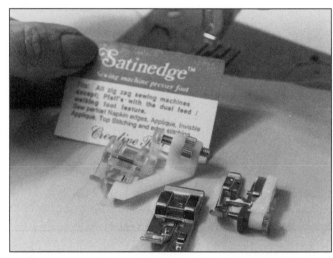

2. You may stabilize the fabric by brushing Perfect Sew stabilizer along the edge. Allow time for the fabric to dry properly or aid drying with the use of a hair dryer. Tear-away stabilizer may also be used.

3. Align the raw edge of the fabric with the right side of the needle opening. Adjust the machine for a satin stitch width of 3 mm– 5 mm and a dense stitch length.

4. The pin of the foot will prevent tunneling the stitched edge.

SEQUENCE 39—SCALLOPING

1. A convenient stabilizer for scalloping the edge of fabric is adding machine tape. Position the tape in your lap, and allow the tape to unroll as you sew. The scallops can be positioned on a raw edge, or along a fold. Trim off excess fabric from the back when the edge is folded over.

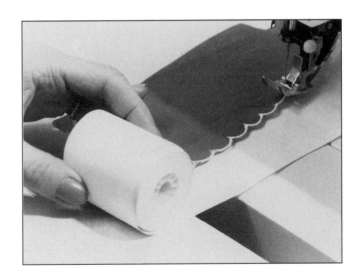

1. The appliqué is positioned on a base fabric with a glue stick or a fusible webbing product. The appliqué and the background are covered with a layer of sheer fabric. The stitch is even with the edge of the appliqué, and sewn through all the layers simultaneously. The stitch shown is a buttonhole, or pin stitch. This is sufficient to prevent fraying while adding a decorative accent to the work. Stabilize your work according to the fabric weight.

1. This attractive edge is suitable for lingerie and lightweight knits. Select the blindstitch formed of four straight stitches and one zigzag. Mirror-image the stitch, if your machine has this option, for the straight stitches to fall to the left of the needle, and the zigzag to swing to the right. Your machine may have this formation without the need of engaging a mirror-image option. Fold the edge over to the wrong side about ½" and sew. Trim away the excess fabric.

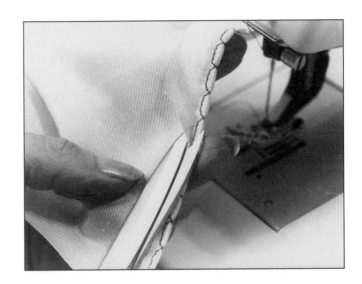

2. On the right side, the zigzag draws the edge in to create a subtle scallop or shell. Use thread to match the color of your fabric. (Contrasting thread was used in the sample for photographic purposes.) Increase the needle tension for a more defined shell formation.

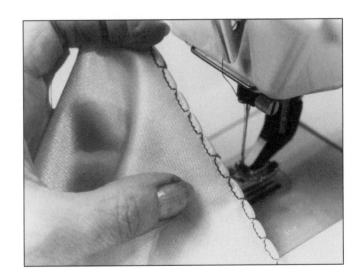

1. Methods vary for machine smocking. A common approach is to load the bobbin with elastic thread and draw up the gathers created with this thread. Rows are sewed parallel but the gathers formed fail to be even. With Stitch 'n' Stretch elastic, the result imitates hand smocking.

2. Commonly used for elastic waistbands, this tape is available in 1½" and 2½" widths. Use two lengths of the 2½" wide tape, each with four rows of elastic, for this procedure. Overlap the first and last row of the bands to create an odd number of seven rows. Remove the elastic from the top row of the second band before overlapping.

3. Sew on all the blue lines of the tape.

4. Remove the elastic from the second, fourth, and sixth row as shown. This area will be reserved for embroidery.

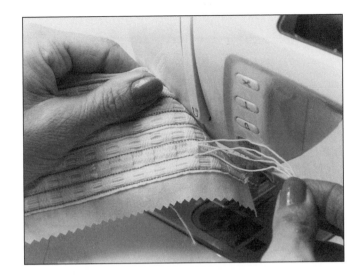

5. Pull the elastic to the size required for the garment under construction.

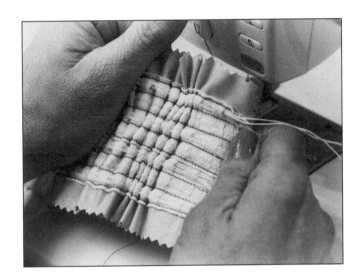

6. The rows of pleats can be evenly adjusted throughout the band. When satisfied with the distribution of pleats, stitch along the elastic edge within the seamline to anchor the threads.

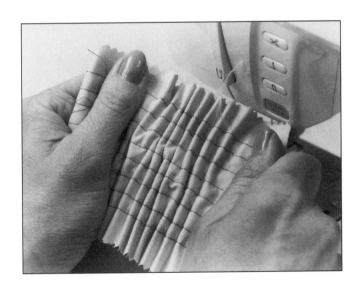

7. Working on the right side of the garment, embroider a satin-formed decorative stitch in the rows that are free of elastic. You will be sewing over the gathers set by the tape.

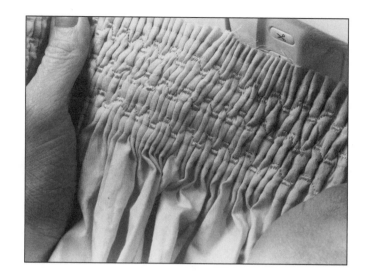

8. Experiment with a variety of satin stitches beyond the traditional ones that imitate hand work. The sample shown was stitched on Baby Lock's Esante sewing machine.

9. Lace can be attached to the edge before attaching a yoke or collar. The completed garment shown in this photograph was embellished with rosebuds which were attached with a button program, and the yoke was stitched by the Pfaff 7550.

1. Select stretch needles and polyester thread that will complement the fabric. Use a stretch stitch on your machine.

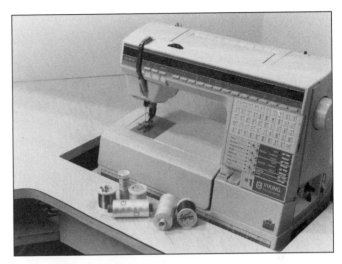

2. If your machine has a limited selection of stretch stitches, a narrow zigzag with a stitch width of 1.5 mm or less will always be appropriate for seaming a knit fabric.

3. Stabilize the fabric to reduce stretch, as the feed dogs and presser feet can distort the fabric during construction.

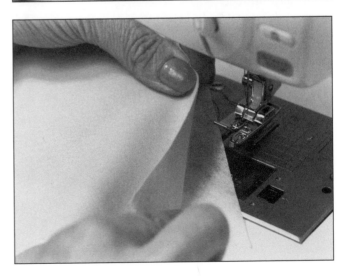

4. Shoulder seams, necklines, and seams prone to stress can be reinforced by the application of Seams Great. This is a ½" precut nonbias strip of nylon tricot. Stitching this band into the seams during construction will stabilize the seams and eliminate stretching during construction and wear.

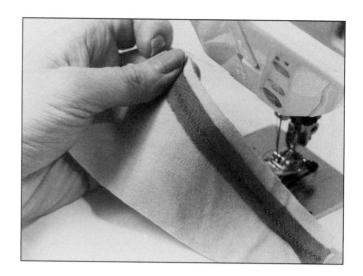

SEQUENCE 44—TOPSTITCHING

1. Use a presser foot that provides a seam guide when topstitching. The foot on the right is a Pfaff blind-hem/edge foot with an adjustable wheel. This foot will fit low-shank machines that accept snap-on feet. The wheel can be set to ride along the fabric edge. The foot held has a convenient indexed metric gauge that can be set at various distances to the fabric edge. This presser foot is made by Brothers and is available at Brothers and Baby Lock dealerships. It will fit low-shank machines that take snap-on feet.

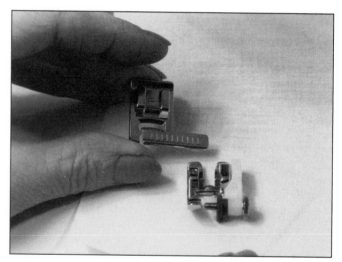

2. Use one of the etched lines on the foot to maintain an even distance from the edge.

3. Parallel rows are easily accomplished with the gauged foot. Align a groove on the gauge along the fabric edge. Maintain this position during sewing. Sew a second pass of stitching, moving the fabric edge to a new groove, or position a groove on a previous sewing line. To sew straight lines you must learn to focus not on the needle but on another reference point during sewing.

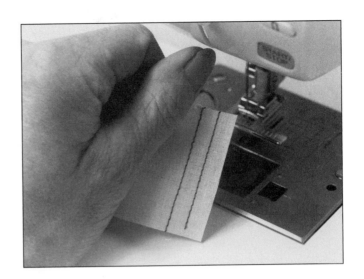

SEQUENCE 45—ZIPPERS

1. Use the zipper foot when applying zippers. The foot held adjusts for left- or right-side seaming by sliding the bar on the back. The zipper foot on the right relies on the needle position changing to the right or left side. Both will bring the seamline close to the zipper teeth.

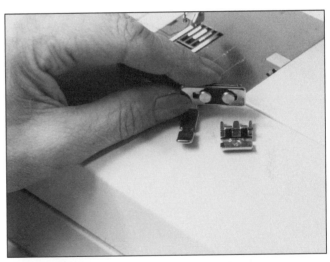

2. When inserting a zipper into a seam, begin by basting the seam closed.

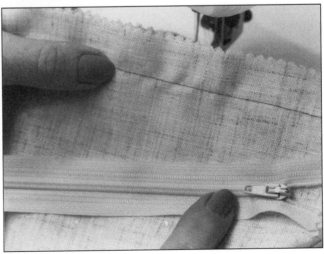

3. Select a zipper longer than the opening to keep the zipper pull out of your sewing path as you work. Attach the left side with the zipper centered on the seam. Keep the zipper in place by pinning or basting to reduce layer shift.

4. Sew across the zipper bottom edge, and complete attaching the left side of the zipper.

5. Remove the basting threads, and slide the zipper pull down.

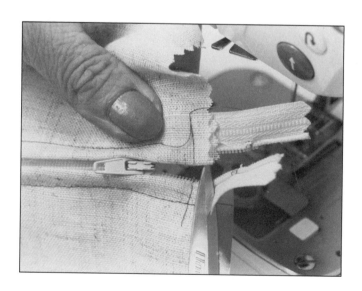

6. Sew across the top edge of the zipper. This will serve as a stop so the zipper ends can be cut off as shown.

7. The wrong side of the zipper tape has a line showing the seamline. This is a guide, but with heavy weight fabrics this line does not ensure an even seam. Baste the zipper on the wrong side, and sew on the right side of the garment to keep the zipper centered. Position the quilting bar centered on the zipper teeth as you sew both zipper sides. The completed zipper assembly shown here was sewn in this manner and embellished with embroidery on the Singer Quantum XL-100.

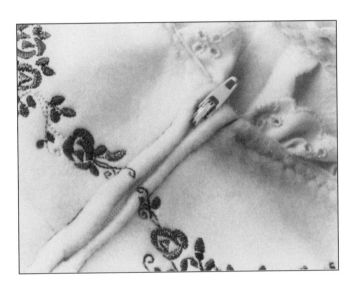

Bibliography

Hazen, Gale Grigg. *Owner's Guide to Sewing Machines, Sergers, and Knitting Machines.* Chilton Book Company, Radnor, Pennsylvania 1989

Henry, Maxine. *The A-Z of The Sewing Machine.* B. T. Batsford Ltd, London 1994

Sew News, Editor Linda Turner Grientrog, Box 3134, Harlan, Iowa 51537

Sewing Update, Editor Cindy Kacynski, PO Box 5026, Harlan, Iowa 51537

The Creative Machine, Editor Robbie Fanning, Open Chain Publishing, PO Box 2634-NL, Menlo Park, California 94026-2634

Threads, Editor Christine Timmons, Taunton Press, PO Box 5506, Newtown, Connecticut 06470

Index